Henry Sturcke
Those Elusive True Values

Those Elusive True Values

Journey to the Center of the Armstrong World

Henry Sturcke

Copyright ©2020 Henry Sturcke
All rights reserved

No part of this book may be reproduced in any form or by any electronic or mechanical means including information storage and retrieval systems without written permission from the author. The only exception is by a reviewer, who may quote short excerpts in a review.

Photo on front cover by Henry Sturcke

ISBN 978-3-952-52270-7 (hardcover)
ISBN 978-3-952-52271-4 (paperback)

Prelude

The book you hold in your hands continues the story that I began in *Fooled into Thinking: Dylan, the Sixties, and the End of the World.*

In that book, I explored how I, a teenage baby boomer, became fascinated by the message of a small church with an oversized public outreach program, the Worldwide Church of God. At the same time, I was gripped by music, especially the songs of Bob Dylan.

Both obsessions took root in the course of one fateful weekend, the days that followed the assassination of John F. Kennedy. I was fifteen years old, a high school sophomore in the suburbs of the New York metropolitan area, and suddenly the world made no sense.

The oscillation between the twin poles of Bible and Dylan continued as I went through high school and enrolled in an urban university; it culminated in the paradox of committing to Worldwide through baptism by immersion and then, four months later, attending the Woodstock music festival.

In this book, the spiritual journey continues, taking me to the center of the church's activity, the campus of Ambassador College in Pasadena, Calif. There I met the church's founder, Herbert Armstrong, and his flamboyant son, Garner Ted, at the time approaching the peak of his influence as a pioneering televangelist. Along with hundreds of fellow students, I soaked up the church's teachings and strove to prepare to play my own part in the outreach of the church.

Midway through my time in Pasadena, Worldwide experienced disconfirmation of its interpretation of Bible prophecy and entered a period of upheaval. Yet I remained a true believer. I thought I had reached my goal and that my search had reached its conclusion. The reality was otherwise, as this book shows.

Chapter One

It was the palm trees that first made me, a life-long east-coaster, feel that I had now reached the other edge.

I had woken early in my home in suburban New Jersey, twenty miles from Manhattan. My parents had driven me to Newark Airport for my flight to Los Angeles. Landing at LAX after watching the brown, mostly-empty continent pass below gave me the first inkling of dislocation from my past. The brazen power of the sunlight as I stepped out of the terminal didn't just illuminate objects, it seemed to have a physical presence of its own. But airports—with glaring sun baking remorselessly through kerosene fumes—tend to resemble; I focused on finding the hotel shuttle to Pasadena.

My destination was Ambassador College, a small coed school in Pasadena maintained by the Worldwide Church of God. When I arrived, I learned my dorm assignment, received my key, and settled into my room. By now, it was late afternoon; I went outside to explore.

That's when it hit. It was the palm trees lining West Del Mar Boulevard that convinced me I was in another place. Rough trunks as sturdy as elephant legs with pineapple hide, gently curved by decades of prevailing winds, topped with tufts of fronds rattling in the breeze, they towered over my dorm and other nearby buildings. I was no longer on the East Coast. A page had irrevocably turned; a new chapter in my life had begun.

My plane might as well have flown over the Himalayas rather than the Rockies and deposited me in Shangri-La. I had entered an enchanted world. Behind my dorm, flowers in all colors and fragrances filled L-shaped beds and hung from trellises over the walkways. Wooden benches beckoned me to linger, but I continued my exploration.

I looked back at my dorm, Manor Del Mar. Something about it seemed familiar. Later, I learned it was a replica of Sagamore Hill, Teddy Roosevelt's estate in New York. I crossed Grove Street (both Grove and its cross-street, Terrace, were closed to traffic, giving the campus a private feel) and approached the library, the building that had once housed the entire college. The college's opening in 1947, twenty-three years earlier, had been delayed until October. In the meantime, most of those who had hoped to attend made other plans.

Through that self-selection, the original quartet was a zealous lot, and Ambassador College could boast of an enviable ratio of eight faculty to four students. I had been born during that first year of the college.

Below the library, to the east, I passed a sunken garden with a shallow reflecting pool and a colonnade. I continued north on Terrace to the sloping dichondra lawns in front of a trio of erstwhile mansions. Fortunes amassed in the Gilded Age had allowed each owner to imagine himself in another time and place. In this fairy tale world, Tudor England bordered Renaissance Tuscany. The most spectacular of these, third in the row, was so quintessentially a mansion that its facade had graced the opening of each week's televised episode of the *Millionaire* in the early fifties.

Herbert Armstrong, the college's founder, had come along when these buildings had sunken in luster. Two had become boarding houses, and a third was scheduled for demolition to make room for lucrative garden apartments. One after the other, Armstrong acquired them for the college. The first two served as women's dorms, while the third, renamed Ambassador Hall, housed classrooms and music studios.

The facades looked familiar, but it surprised me to see how close together they stood. Previously, I had seen them only in lush photos in the *Envoy*, the college's yearbook. The sumptuous 1969 edition had featured double-paged spreads of highly detailed shots of these buildings, taken with an 8-by-10 camera and wide-angle lens. The effect of the lens distortion, I now realized, was larger-than-life.

Nevertheless, I was happy to be here at last. I never walked such thoroughly landscaped grounds before. The gurgling rock stream descending the lawn between Mayfair and Terrace Villa refreshed me.

It wasn't merely the beauty of buildings and grounds that impressed me. I had yearned to attend Ambassador College for years. Like many young people that summer, I headed west in search of spiritual enlightenment. While some sat at the feet of Ram Dass or other gurus, I had flown to a gleaming campus where the men sported short haircuts and the women wore knee-length skirts.

Five years earlier, while my high school classmates were making plans to apply for prestigious colleges and universities, most of them in the Northeast, I had believed the accolades this college heaped on itself in the pages of the *Plain Truth* magazine. I had no idea how to differentiate Harvard from Yale or Williams from Swarthmore, but the slogans of this college's founder, Herbert Armstrong, appealed to me. "Recapturing True Values." "Teaching not only how to earn a living, but how to live." The former adman had a gift for the resonant phrase.

The *Plain Truth*, along with a broadcast, the *World Tomorrow*, posed as an extension program of the college but were actually a mission of the Worldwide Church of God (as the Radio Church of God had recently renamed itself). This became clear to me as I read on, and so I aspired not only to attend the college but to become a member.

My parents had reservations, and I conceded that it would be wise to begin at a recognized school to have a basis of comparison. I went to Boston University's School of Public Communication (SPC) to acquire skills I could use in the outreach of the church. Sixteen months before flying to California, I became a member through baptism by immersion (my first baptism, as an infant, in the Lutheran church, was not valid in the eyes of Worldwide).

Because I had remained in Boston for all four years, rather than transfer to Ambassador after one, I thought I had missed my chance to attend. I was happy to be in the church, but no longer thought of attending Ambassador. That soon changed.

An Ambassador student, Dean, was home for the summer of 1969, soon after my baptism, and attended services in the Boston congregation (which actually met nearby in transcendent Concord). He invited me to visit him one weekend, so we drove to his home on Cape Cod after services. During a walk on the beach, I asked him about college life, and he asked me why I didn't enter. I told of my not applying three years earlier, and said: "I'm not sure God wants me there now."

His reply was immediate and forceful: "Well, if he does, he's not going to send you an engraved invitation. You'll have to apply like everyone else."

So, I applied, and now I had arrived. It seemed like paradise on earth as I circled back and returned to my dorm.

Manor Del Mar was the farthest from classrooms, but the campus was compact, so that had nothing to do with my chronic last-minute rush to class over the next three years. The ground-floor of Del Mar featured a lounge, with richly upholstered seating and exotic wood paneling that contradicted the ordinary meaning of "lounge." It was even less inviting for lounging than the formal living rooms of many of my high school classmates. Beyond that lay study cubicles and sleeping rooms, with more upstairs on the second floor.

Above that, there was an attic. That was where I had been assigned, one of ten students. There was one room for our desks, and another room had just enough space for five sets of bunk beds. In addition to the study area and the shared bedroom, there was a shower room on the north end of the building. To the south, there was storage space in a west-facing alcove off the bedroom that had been converted to prayer closets, each with a stool handy for spreading open a Bible or prayer lists as one knelt. There was one other feature of that wing, a small door that led to a tiny iron balcony. I often took my Bible there. I found it easier to commune with the divine overlooking the trellised garden, enjoying regular visits from hummingbirds sampling the nectar of the flowers growing up the wall, than in a stuffy, sound-proofed closet.

One by one, I met my roommates. One of them, Hal, spotting my camera bag, recognized a kindred spirit, and took me in hand. That evening, he invited me to come along with him and two coeds to the Salt Shaker, a favorite after-dinner hangout of the students. I had been ready to call it a day; I had awoken long ago and far away, but I let myself be persuaded. It soon became apparent that Hal and one of the coeds were a couple, involved, in the college sociolect. That led to my introduction to the dating rules, meant to manage more than 500 young men and women so that as many as possible could graduate, with as few pregnancies as possible and a minimum of broken hearts. One rule was no more than two dates per semester with a given person. A second was: Beginning with the junior year, that could be upped to three times a semester. In senior year, as preparation for marriage, somewhat more. There were ways around the rules, however. (On this double date, for instance, I escorted Hal's sweetheart that evening.)

Hal was from the Pacific Northwest and had grown up in the church. Too much farm work when he was too young left him with a bad back and a jaundiced view of life, or what the administration termed a "bad attitude," another key phrase in the college idiom. To the higher-ups, it was already clear that Hal was not "field" material (another bit of college idiom, denoting a candidate for ordination), so his future, if he managed to avoid being kicked out, would be to serve in one of the supporting services. As it turned out, he went on to excel as one of several talented photographers for the Worldwide's publications in years to come.

It was fortunate that Hal was the first friend I made in Pasadena. His experience of the gap between Worldwide's proclaimed ideals and their sometimes less-than-ideal application was a helpful counterbalance to my utopian view.

I was one of 150 incoming students arriving that day from all parts of the U.S. and Canada. Some had grown up in Worldwide dreaming for years of Ambassador College as the promised land. Other church-grown youths would have rather gone somewhere else, but their parents wanted them here. For a few, the attraction of Ambassador was its proximity to Hollywood, Sunset Strip, or the beach. A few already lived in Southern California and were not enthused about the move from the comforts of home to a dorm.

Others of us were relatively new in the church. We were the dreamers. Our experiences of "the world" had convinced us there must be something better. More than a few of us had attended another college, and some, like myself, had graduated. We had been overwhelmed or repulsed by the panoply of possibilities of the Sixties. Yet for me, and others, there was at the same time a romantic tug toward what the youth movement represented, as one book at the time defined it, the counter culture.

Among those entering Pasadena with me were the first unmarried African-American students at Ambassador. Until then, because of Worldwide's stand against interracial dating, only married African-American students could attend, but the proportion of blacks in the ministry was much smaller than the proportion of black members in the congregations, including the congregations I was familiar with in the Boston and New York metropolitan areas. Integrated congregations were one of the things I enjoyed most about my new allegiance. Now, we were told, since the need for workers was great and time was short, it was time to open the doors to single black students. The college admitted an equal number of black men and women, ten in all. The rule against interracial dating, however, remained in place, even though—unlike the other dating rules—it was never mentioned in the student handbook.

I already knew one of them, Yolette, from Harlem. My friend Frank in Boston was sweet on her, but with college now as a possibility, there was no chance for him. I always enjoyed her bright, quirky nature, and was happy she would attend with me.

I was surprised that another was not there, my friend Murdock. He began attending the Boston congregation a few months after I did. He was from Tuskegee, Ala., and a freshman at Brandeis, but dreamt of attending Ambassador. I spent many hours with Murdock, talking and sharing our mutual love of music-making. He was an extremely talented pianist with a good voice. In the words of a Sly Stone song, to each other, we were just everyday people.

I knew he had applied to Ambassador, so after a few months in Pasadena, I asked someone in the administration why he had been rejected. He told me that Murdock had listed Martin Luther King, Jr., as a person he admired on his application (confidentiality was not a strong suit at the college). The admissions committee decided the college didn't want to accept any revolutionaries. In the coming years, Murdock continued to demonstrate his commitment to the church in the Boston area and finally was accepted the fifth time he applied. His first year in college coincided with my last year, but he attended a sister campus of the college, in Big Sandy, Tex., where he quickly became known as Doc. That campus integrated the year after Pasadena did. Church officials had feared that an integrated student body in rural East Texas might be a provocation, but now their hand was forced. In the fall of 1970, the U.S. government revoked tax-exempt status from Bob Jones University in South Carolina over its racial policy, which was similar to Ambassador's, based on the same Biblical understanding.

When I compare my first days in Pasadena with my first in Boston, four years earlier, I'm surprised at how I allowed myself to be cocooned in the campus. California exerted a magnetic pull on us baby boomers. The songs we heard on the radio celebrated sports cars and surfing in a way that made life there seem like an extended summer vacation. As the music matured, it exuded good vibrations of every kind. My lack of curiosity about the world beyond the periphery of the college's forty-five-acre campus strikes me as curious now. In Boston, I had begun to explore both that city and Cambridge across the river the day I arrived. Why didn't I go check out the Troubador, as I had Club 47 and the Unicorn? In fact, I hadn't even brought a guitar.

Instead, I stayed on campus. The busy round of placement tests, voice auditions, course registration, and receiving job assignments didn't leave much time for exploration anyway.

The social highlight of the week was the faculty reception on Thursday evening. Men in white dinner jackets and black ties, faculty wives and coeds in gowns, all gathered on the plaza of the Academic Center, bounded by the rear facade of Ambassador Hall and two recently-built classroom buildings with honey-combed facades. The fourth side of the plaza was open to the west, where, through the spray of cascading fountains in a reflecting pool, the soft colors of a Southern California twilight were fading beyond South Orange Grove Boulevard. We incoming students were nervous and eager to make a good impression.

When my turn came in the receiving line, I shook hands with Herbert Armstrong for the first time, after seven years of absorbing his writings. His daughter Beverly stood at his side, acting in the role of hostess. His full-moon face assumed a warm, friendly expression, but his most appealing physical feature were his hands. They were large in proportion to the rest of his short, portly body, and gracefully shaped.

While his personality continued to dominate the college, we saw less of him than students had in the first two decades of the college's existence. Armstrong's wife Loma had died a little over three years earlier, in spring 1967. As classes resumed in the fall of 1970, it was the first time without any undergraduates who had been students when she died.

Soon after Loma's death, close associates urged him to travel as a way of dealing with his grief and loss. He became a globe-trotter in his private Gulfstream II executive jet, visiting prime ministers, kings, even emperors, accompanied by a small group of advisors and facilitators. Since the "Work" (the always-capitalized term that encompassed college, church, and public proclamation) was an entrepreneurial start-up, an extension of this one man, it lacked a long institutional history and had an organization that defied simple charting since almost all leading executives had three or more job titles. Access to Herbert Armstrong was the crucial factor for the making and unmaking of decisions. Those traveling with him had that access.

So, after welcoming us, he left on Sunday morning to fly to the church's two other campuses in Big Sandy, Tex., and Bricket Wood, England. From there, he embarked on a round-the-world tour with stops in India, Singapore, the Philippines, and Japan. Directly after that, he planned to visit gatherings of the church in France, England, and throughout the U.S. and Canada for the eight-day Feast of Tabernacles. In all, he would be gone four-to-five weeks.

We incoming students exchanged pleasantries with other faculty members. One who made an impression was Roderick C. Meredith, whose name was known to me through articles and booklets. After joining the church, I learned that he was the director of Church Administration, and therefore supervisor of all the ministry. He was one of the church's evangelists. The ministry was organized in a way that mixed New Testament terminology (apostle, evangelist, pastor, elder, deacon) with a military-style organizational structure. These offices were ranks; an evangelist outranked a pastor in the same way that a general outranked a colonel. The only one who outranked Rod Meredith was Herbert Armstrong himself, styled an apostle, and Herbert's son, Garner Ted, first among equals among the evangelists.

Meredith preached and wrote in an intense, hectoring way. But in person, the tense energy he exuded was combined with a bashful boyish smile. He was interested to learn I had been at B.U. The recently retired president there was, it turned out, from Meredith's home town of Joplin, Mo., and the two families were acquainted. He was even more interested when I let it slip out that I had for the last six months been the second man on visits two or three times a week. Something I had been cautioned, before leaving for college, not to mention.

Why not?

Much of a field minister's work week was spent on the road, visiting members and "prospective members," Worldwide's term for people who had written to Pasadena after having their interest piqued by the media and print outreach of the church. My own first personal contact with the church had come about that way, when the pastor of the recently-established New England congregation came to my dorm room in the spring of 1967, accompanied by another man, who I later learned was a deacon in the local area. When the pastor returned for a second visit, his sidekick was a recent graduate of the Bricket Wood campus, sent to him for training prior to ordination.

It was Worldwide's policy that visiting teams went out in twos. The basis for this was in the Gospels, when Jesus first sent out the twelve in pairs (Mark 6:7). The practice proved valuable in many ways. Some of those who requested visits were women living on their own, and they might have felt more comfortable having two coming to visit than one man alone; at the very least, it protected the reputation of all involved. Sometimes the prospective had a mate who was displeased with this new enthusiasm of his or her partner; thus, safety in numbers. Serving as a second man on a visit was valuable training for recent graduates who were candidates for ordination, and also for local men who might serve as deacons or elders.

But one thing was frowned upon: using a college applicant in this role. Although the college had been started so that Herbert Armstrong could train helpers in his ministry, he was allergic to anyone who entered with the idea of becoming a minister. This might sound as illogical as the idea of someone entering dental college but denying that he wanted to become a dentist, but it was Armstrong's conviction, based on his early experiences, that some of those convinced they had a calling to preach were the last he wished to see in that role. Thus, the antithetical policy of having a college with only one major, theology, but only accepting students who disavowed any intention of becoming a minister.

This only applied to the male half of the student body since the church did not ordain women. Thus, women who took the same program as the men graduated with a degree in religion, rather than theology. The coeds could either look forward to becoming the wife of a minister or working as a secretary in one of the departments of the Work.

Regardless of how the administration generally felt about college applicants serving on visits, Meredith remained friendly in our conversation. Perhaps he made a mental note to look into why the local minister had taken me along, but his demeanor didn't change.

Chapter Two

So how was it that I had spent the months before entering Ambassador on the visiting program, beginning less than a year after my baptism and three years after the first visit I had received?

I passed my high school and college years oscillating between two influences: literature published by this college in Pasadena, and the music of Bob Dylan. I immersed myself in both on the somber weekend after the Kennedy assassination, repeatedly playing Dylan's LP *Freewheelin'* while devouring a stack of *Plain Truth* magazines. This primitive-looking monthly related current events to the church's interpretation of Bible prophecy. At times, the message of each was in diametrical opposition to the other. At other times, they seemed to share a common perception that the world was on its last legs and that a hard rain, as in the days of Noah, was indeed a-gonna fall.

In the spring of 1969, I took the decisive step of breaking up with my fiancée and accepting baptism by immersion into the church behind the *Plain Truth*, the Worldwide Church of God. The commitment this entailed formed a counterpoint to my final year at Boston University.

An eloquent expression of this was the August weekend that saw me both attending Sabbath worship service (Worldwide observed the seventh-day) and the music festival at Woodstock.

Amid the romantic and spiritual upheaval, I earned my best grade point average in that spring semester of my junior year. I intended to continue in this vein as I began my senior year. Within weeks, however, my new commitment to the church overwhelmed my scholastic resolve. As the semester progressed, classes diminished in importance compared to a rigorous routine of daily prayer and Bible study. I attended services every Saturday morning, followed by invitations to the homes of other members or leisurely lunches at a Howard Johnson's restaurant between Concord and Boston (my car was filled with most of the other members who lived in Boston). In addition, there were weekly Bible studies on Wednesday evening, and a training club for men based on the Toastmasters program, called Spokesman's Club, on Tuesday night.

Of all my studies, the only one I didn't neglect was photography, both the classes toward my degree and my assignments for the weekly school newspaper.

The third semester of photojournalism aimed at creating reportage. Oscar and Karen, friends I had met through my former fiancée, Sian, agreed to let me do a photo-essay about them. It was a dramatic time in their lives; Karen, pregnant with their second child, sensed Oscar's ambivalence about getting married. In the time I covered them, the baby was born but had to remain in the hospital, where I spent time with them, as well as in their brownstone in Boston's South End. The photos came out well, the low-light conditions in which I took them added a gritty, documentary feel. I worked hard at getting good prints and writing the accompanying text.

Our teacher, Harris Smith, was incredulous. When it came time to share our projects with the class, he asked: "Did you do this?" I didn't mind that his remarks reflected unkindly on my work until then; it was a satisfying moment. I was in awe of many of the other photographers in our class and happy that I finally produced a project that could also earn Smith's respect.

Soon after that, the publisher of a photography magazine, *San Francisco Camera*, contacted him and proposed a sister publication, *East Coast Camera*, and asked Smith if his students would like to produce the first issue. We agreed, and the group settled on me as one of two of us to edit it. I enjoyed the group spirit as the entire class worked together, helping each other choose his or her best photos and sharing advice about getting the best print. My contribution evoked a second surprised reaction from Smith, and at a conference after the project was finished, he speculated that my strength might lie in editing, rather than in writing or photography.

One more thing fell by the wayside that year: my poetry. I had started to respond to it in high school; my interest deepened as I became exposed to more of the best in my college classes. In my junior year, I went to the Brookline public library regularly, checked out a stack of the most recent collections—Silkin, Levertov, Merwin, and others—and read through one each night in bed before falling asleep.

I had been starting to get somewhere with my own writing, then it went away. One speaks of having inspiration dry up, but in my case, it would be more appropriate to say I choked it off. First lines often came to me shortly after falling into a melancholic state. These purple aura moments often meant that I became less aware of my surroundings and let words come. I remember a time I began to fall into this state after my baptism while riding in a car filled with church members. We were driving on a minor highway somewhere in New England. I was sitting in the front passenger seat, and as the light and shade of the fall foliage flashed past me, I began to drift into that familiar mood, at once hyper-observant and disassociated, tinged with melancholy. I willfully fought off the frame of mind, telling myself to remain "outgoing," interested in the others sharing the ride with me. Worldwide encouraged "fellowship" while exuding a latent suspicion of creative minds. To out oneself as a poet would have been akin to confessing a moral failing. The warnings from the pulpit about demon-influence pertained: picture the moody loner in his garret agonizing over just the right word. And so, as we drove, I willed myself to exhibit the fruit of the spirit. One fruit the Apostle Paul mentions, joy, seemed to be the opposite of the purple aura. Over the next few months, its visits became rarer.

A few weeks after the fall semester began, I left Boston to attend a church festival for the first time. A year earlier, I had learned that Worldwide, in addition to the weekly Sabbath, also observed the annual Holy Days outlined in the Old Testament. Most of them were observed in local congregations, but one, the Feast of Tabernacles (Sukkoth), was different.

The observance of Tabernacles, in the fall, was the Church's counterpoint to its rejection of the common Christian celebrations, such as Easter and Christmas. Leaning heavily on the teachings of the "history of religion" school of the early twentieth century, Worldwide insisted that such days were pagan. My literature study offered corroboration, for Frazier's *Golden Bough* was essential for understanding much twentieth-century poetry.

A side effect of the non-observance of Easter and Christmas was that it distanced us from our families since these days were not only religious observances but also occasions for family reunions.

My discovery of the Biblical feasts had exposed me to some good-natured teasing from Sian, my fiancée, in our final months together. In the *Peanuts* comics we both loved, Linus proselytized his allegiance to the Great Pumpkin, whose return in the fall (the time of Tabernacles) Linus faithfully awaits. A small doubt flickered in me, and I wondered whether I weren't being as naïve as Linus. But my father had raised me to always consider there could be another side to any issue and not to be afraid to take a minority stance. It was indisputable that the majority wasn't always right. After all, the majority supported the Vietnam War.

And so, my knowledge that the entire membership of the church (some 60,000 at the time) gathered at locations around the world for this eight-day celebration intensified my yearning to become a part of the church. Now that I was officially a member, I could attend.

I spent most of the night before leaving in the darkroom to finish assignments; I would miss more than a week of classes while away. After settling into a deep slumber in the early hours of the morning, it seemed as if no time had passed when I became aware of urgent knocking on my door. I had slept through my alarm clock, and my passengers to the Feast were worried about being late.

We drove to the Poconos in eastern Pennsylvania, where the church had built its own tabernacle: a large field house, with concrete floor and bridge and girder system holding up the metal roof. I never asked whether the property had previously been a pumpkin patch. By the time I dropped each of my passengers at his or her lodgings, found the inn where I had rented a room, then drove to the tabernacle for the opening evening service, I was late. The parking lot was filled with a thousand or more cars, and the only spaces left were a long way from the building.

My self-recrimination at being late gave way to exhilaration as I walked in. I had missed the opening hymns, and a speaker already stood on the large stage. It was Rod Meredith, whose name was familiar to me as one of the main writers in the *Plain Truth*.

When the hymn-singing resumed, I experienced the thrill of adding my voice to ten thousand others. Two months earlier, I had been one of a throng, half-a-million strong, in Woodstock. Now, amid glorious fall foliage, I experienced a similar sense of community, or shared purpose, albeit on a smaller scale.

The rest of the week-long feast whizzed by. Bible instructions for how to observe it are sparse: Israelites were to dwell in booths (Sukkoth); these temporary dwellings served as a reminder of the forty years in the wilderness following the exodus from Egypt. The church's adaptation of this was that rented rooms in an inn, a motel, or even vacation condos were "temporary dwellings." Rather than focus on events thousands of years in the past, the

24

feast was interpreted as a foretaste of the imminent future when, after the return of Jesus Christ to put an end to war, the Millennium—or, in the phrase of the Armstrongs, the "wonderful world tomorrow"—would begin. Worldwide rejected the mainstream conception of heaven and expected in its place that the Kingdom of God would be brought to earth at Jesus' return. The Millennium (Latin for "thousand years," the time mentioned in Rev. 20:5, when the resurrected saints would rule with Christ) would inaugurate this. Ironically, my high school bandmate, Mike Fennelly, had gone to California and was now part of a songwriting and recording collective that its founder, Curt Boettcher, also named the Millennium, as an expression of his utopian hopes.

To help us feast-goers get in the spirit of this soon-to-be time of peace and prosperity, we had saved ten percent of our income. Having ten percent of your gross earnings to spend in eight days, roughly two percent of the year, meant that we lived on a higher standard than at home. Restaurants in the area got into the spirit of it; they were informed of our dietary preferences. Our adherence to the teachings of the Torah meant no pork. When I went to breakfast the first morning and ordered eggs, the waitress asked if I wanted bacon with it. I said no thanks, but she quickly informed me it was beef bacon, which I hadn't known existed.

The main portion of our observance, though, was a mix

of tent revival and Chautauqua assembly (think pre-internet TED-talks). Each morning and afternoon, we gathered at the tabernacle for two-hour services. The format was the same as the weekly services I attended back in Massachusetts, but everything was on a larger scale. I dutifully took notes in the comb-bound feast brochure. Both Herbert Armstrong and his son Garner Ted jetted in for a service each, bringing an elevated sense of excitement. When Herbert Armstrong visited, the first shorter message, the "sermonette," was given by Stanley R. Rader, an attorney and accountant who accompanied Herbert Armstrong on all his trips. His dry speaking style contrasted with all the others who spoke that week.

A third component of the feast experience was volunteer labor. Our congregation's assignment was the early morning set-up—aligning chairs and other light maintenance. The second morning, I rose early and drove over with others. We stopped at a diner on the way. Eating my scrambled egg sandwich, I felt like one of the guys. I felt even better that my crew chief, from a small town in Vermont, had three attractive daughters, two of whom were still living at home and were there in the Poconos with their parents. The older of the two, June, had attended the college's Big Sandy campus the previous year but did not return for a second year. The younger, Doreen, was a high school senior. I spent most of the little free time between services with them.

Having the entire membership gathered in a few locations was handy for Ambassador in recruiting the next year's incoming class. Interested candidates sat for a battery of tests. A friendly young fellow from Pittsburgh, Wayne, sat next to me and struck up a conversation. I later learned that two of his brothers were ministers, but Wayne was very down-to-earth (it turned out that his brothers Dave and Gary were, too, as I got to know them). The college sent representatives to each site to conduct interviews with prospective students. Lynn Torrance, the registrar at Big Sandy, attended in the Poconos. He struck me as gruff (I later learned he was a survivor of the Bataan death march) and acted cool toward me. I told June and Doreen how the interview had gone, and June took me in hand, coaching me on how to present myself and giving my hair a trim. She also engineered a spontaneous re-meet with Dr. Torrance between services a couple of days later, and after a short chat, he said that his second impression of me was much better than his first.

I returned home with a college application, which I filled out and submitted. Two questions on it gave me pause, but I decided to answer them honestly. One was about drug use, the other asked for my favorite television show. It was the second of them that I was more worried might damage my chances. For years, I had hardly watched any television, but recently *Sesame Street* had just debuted on public television (WGBH in Boston), and after one of the SPC professors mentioned it favorably, I watched a couple of episodes and agreed that it was good television. As for the other question, that worried me less; I reasoned that the admissions committee would find it hard to believe that I attended a large eastern university and hadn't experimented, so there was no reason not to be truthful.

Part of the application process was an interview with a "college representative." Now that I was a member, I knew that would be the local minister. Fred Kellers had replaced Reg Platt a few months after my baptism. The church transferred local ministers frequently; few remained longer than five years in an area in those days. Fred and his wife, Lucretia, invited me to their home for my interview. Fred made good use of my visit. All field ministers had to submit up-to-date photos for a church publication, so we hung a sheet for a backdrop and set up lighting. After I took his portrait, he took mine for my application.

As a potential Ambassador student, my participation in Spokesman's Club was encouraged. Club was designed to develop the men (women could not participate) in public speaking and leadership skills. The Boston club was full, but there was an opening in the club in the sister congregation in New Hampshire. I undertook the hour-and-a-half drive through rush hour traffic weekly to the Holiday Inn in Portsmouth, site of the meetings, picking up another Boston member, Steve, along the way. He was a Coast Guard veteran who lived north of Boston. Like me, he was eager to show his commitment.

The club director was John, the English trainee who accompanied Reg Platt on Platt's return visit before inviting me to services in 1967. Since then, John had been ordained, and remained in the area as associate pastor of the two-church circuit, primarily looking after the northern half—Maine, New Hampshire, Vermont, and western Massachusetts.

Despite its claim on my time, I enjoyed club. The first half of the meeting featured, in addition to the minutes of the previous meeting and discussion of old and new business, table topics. Each week, a club member prepared a set of questions that he posed from a lectern at the front of the room. Some were innocuous and humorous, such as whether we preferred briefs or boxer shorts, at least one dealt with current events, and one was a biblical topic (usually a difficult scripture). As soon as the question was posed, hands shot up the air, the member called upon leapt to his feet and answered, followed by others. Those who were shy were called on, whether they raised hands or not, but most were eager to make a good impression on the club director. This meant that the answers were often more zealous than thoughtful.

I noticed that the answers to current events questions often didn't reflect solid information. To remedy this, I introduced a motion one week during new business. I proposed using club money to buy and mount a world map, and then devote a portion of time each week to having members share news items they had brought that had prophetic significance and comparing these with the map. I wasn't aware of it, but I was following the habit of my Civil War veteran great-great-grandfather. My mother later shared her recollection of him in old age as he sat in his rocking chair with radio, newspaper, globe, and Bible in reach. The motion carried, I was told to purchase the map, but the club decided on one additional detail. Members would bring the items, but then I would wrap up their comments with an overall analysis.

After a coffee break, the second half featured five speeches. The club manual contained descriptions and instructions of a series of twelve speeches, adapted from the Toastmaster's manual. The first was an ice-breaker, in which a member told of his life. Other lessons focused on elements such as adding color—usually by loading the speech with superfluous adjectives—or getting the facts. Midway through the program, the sixth assignment called for a motivational speech, a "stir-to-action." This assignment was tricky; while the club director was always on the lookout for candidates who could bring sermonettes (the shorter first message) in weekly services, we were also admonished that no one should set out to be a preacher. The challenge was to motivate but not preach. Many of us had to take more than one shot at that assignment.

An even more difficult assignment lay just ahead, the

seventh assignment, the complete speech, intended to incorporate all the elements of the lessons so far. The dreaded eighth speech was the attack. It might seem that for a group of apocalyptically-minded fundamentalists, there would be no shortage of topics to choose from. The difficulty for many of us was in giving vent to our emotions and to increase the volume of our voices without losing control of ourselves or our material.

Another tricky assignment was the penultimate, the impromptu. Even for those of us who could think quickly on our feet, it was no easy matter to speak in an organized manner for six minutes on a topic announced while you walked to the lectern. The manual offered some useful structures on which to hang our thoughts: past, present, future, for instance, or pro and con. The trick was to recall them while standing in front of the group. Woe to you, however, if you were caught off guard. Normally, you would know a week in advance that you would give an impromptu at the next meeting. But a member could have an impromptu sprung on him without warning as well. Sometimes this could be used in a disciplinary way if a member seemed to be napping or otherwise inattentive. But more often it occurred if one of the assigned speakers did not show up, whether for illness or some other reason. That happened to me one night when our director was absent, and the president, Jim, chaired the meeting. He announced me with no warning, and I barely registered the topic as I walked to the lectern: love. This was ironic, given the re-action that my then-fiancée, Sian, and I had after experi-encing our first service two-and-a-half years earlier. Love was precisely what had been missing in the messages we heard. It is probably just as well that it didn't come to mind to take that tangent. By that time, I had accepted the in-doctrination that love meant keeping the commandments. But I didn't speak in an organized way about that, either. I spent the next six minutes flailing, hectoring the club of our need to show love to one another.

I failed the speech. It was an embarrassing experience, perhaps the low point in a year in which I often took home a trophy for the most effective speech, the most improved speaker, or the most helpful evaluation. We all said that the third trophy was the most-prized since it meant we had helped a fellow member. But secretly, I also enjoyed winning the most effective speech.

With all day Saturday taken care of, as well as two nights a week (we often got back from club so late that I slept on Steve's sofa rather than continue home), there was little time to study for my classes.

That final year brought a change in my living arrange-ments as well. When classes resumed, I still shared an apartment with my friend Andy and a third student, Ron, who replaced the third of our original triumvirate, Char-lie. The hot water boiler broke during the summer and hadn't been repaired when the chill of a New England fall set in. As long as the good weather held, taking cold showers and boiling water to shave was only an inconvenience, but we had already been through three Boston winters and demanded action. After an escalating fight with our landlord, he canceled our lease, and we were out.

Once I returned from the Feast, the search for new lodgings began (our eviction notice had come while I was away). The school year had already started, and few apartments remained on the market. We found one, not as nice as the one we were leaving and at a higher price. I couldn't afford an increase, so Alan, the drummer from the band I was part of in high school, now living in Boston, took my place.

I was loath to ask my parents for more money for increased rent. One reason for this was that they knew I tithed on the pocket money they sent me. Tithing is an old-fashioned word I first learned from the literature of the church. It's old English for "tenth" and refers to the practice in ancient Israel of setting aside a portion of agricultural produce to support the temple and its priesthood. In the third and sixth year of a seven-year cycle, it served the additional purpose of relieving the poor.

In common with other churches, Worldwide taught that this divine law was still in effect, but spiritualized, since no temple stood. Instead, it now served the two purposes of supporting the Work and its ministry, as well as for the expenses of attending the annual festivals. Rather than split the tithe between these two purposes, World-wide taught that there were two tithes, and even a third in the third and sixth year to support the "widows and orphans." Besides, although the tithe in the Old Testament was taken on produce (livestock was handled differently: the first-born was sacrificed), the church taught that this now applied to wages and other income. The word "increase" was understood to mean that those who owned businesses could deduct expenses before calculating tithable income, but wage-earners were not permitted to deduct taxes or expenses. This meant that members set aside twenty to thirty percent of gross income for purposes determined by the church.

This practice made it possible for such a small number of members to finance sending out three million copies of the *Plain Truth* each month, as well as millions of booklets each year. These tithes paid for television and radio time, as well as advertising. Together with inexpensive student labor, they enabled the church to support three resplendent college campuses. Finally, they paid for the expenses to hundreds of local congregations and their pastors, although in those years, the ministry was paid meager wages, making the first fruits given by farmers and gardeners in the congregation very welcome. Also, whenever there was a financial crisis (that is, whenever Herbert Armstrong over-extended the outreach of the church or the building program on the campuses), one of the first measures taken was to withhold wages of the ministers.

Of course, the allowance my parents sent me for rent and food was not money I had earned. Common sense dictated that it was my dad's responsibility to tithe or not on his money, not mine. They generously supported the Lutheran congregation I was brought up in, but since that was no longer a "true church" in my eyes, I felt the money they sent me had not been tithed on, so I decided on my own to do so. Of course, a minister might have admitted to me that I wasn't responsible for doing this, had I asked. But I didn't ask.

Thus, unable to pay more rent, I went on my own and spent many evenings ringing on doorbells, responding to ads. Finally, I inquired about a room in a large house on St. Paul Street in Brookline. The house was owned by an elderly couple from the Maritimes. They rented a spacious room on the ground floor, facing the street. The room had an irregular shape, with a second rectangle jutting off at an angle to form an oriel at the corner of the house. I placed my table in that alcove, the light through the windows (top half stained glass), shaded by a porch, was perfect for reading. I had a private toilet but shared the bath and the kitchen with the couple from whom I rented.

Not only was the light good for reading; I experimented and found I could use it to create good portraits. Drama students had begun hiring me to take photos for their portfolios. This began with one of Sian's friends, Jackie.

She had photos done professionally but wasn't pleased with the results. I had taken some photos in rehearsals of plays she had been in, so she asked me to try my hand. The photos pleased her, she told many of her classmates, and soon I had a welcome supplement to my pocket money. One of the actresses was especially beautiful. She arrived, took out the blouse she wanted to wear for the portraits and started changing; I was embarrassed and quickly ushered her into the privacy of the toilet while I set up my camera and adjusted the curtains. I'm sure I cut a comical figure in my prudishness, but I was careful to avoid any adventures in my new celibacy. When I developed the photos, they were some of the most beautiful I had taken. I made several prints and drove to her apartment to deliver them. She was equally pleased with them and took my hand as she looked through them. I was glad that I had fitted in the delivery while on my way to New Hampshire for Spokesman's Club, and that I had with me another student, Jim, who had begun attending services. It also went through my mind that perhaps she was hoping to pay me in a different way, but I needed the money more.

Nevertheless, money remained tight. My supper was often one boiled potato. Once, I decided to "tithe" my books. I rigorously took one-tenth of the books from my shelves and went across the river to a used bookstore in Cambridge. The store-owner urged me to reconsider one of the books in particular: my first-edition hardback copy of Richard Farina's *Been Down So Long It Looks Like Up to Me.* It was out-of-print, much sought-after, and his store policy would only allow him to give me one-tenth of the original purchase price, a pittance to what the book would go for, three years after appearing. I remained resolute. The thought of Lot's wife flashed through my mind, turning back for one last look at Sodom. I had made up my mind to reduce my possessions, and that's what I did.

Another way I supplemented my pocket money was by working occasional Sundays for a builder in the congregation who sold pre-fabricated homes. It began when he needed one more person for a couple of days to put up drywall in a house in Woodstock, Vt. I took that as a blessing since otherwise, I couldn't have afforded to take Doreen, the youngest of the daughters of my Feast crew chief, to the Ladies' night our Spokesman's Club planned to hold.

One other task remained in the last month of 1969: filing the paperwork for conscientious objector status. In my childhood, as part of my general interest in U.S. history, I had read about the Revolution, the Civil War, in which at least two of my great-great-grandfathers fought (on the losing side), World War II, in which my father had fought, and the other wars. I spent a day visiting West Point and thought of becoming a cadet. In my three years of high school, the country became mired in a war whose aims were less clear-cut; increasingly, it seemed unwinnable. The two classmates with whom I trained guerrilla war tactics in high school both ended up there. Another class-mate, who enlisted in the Marines right after graduation, was dead three months later, shortly after arriving in Vietnam.

Boston, with several colleges in the area, was a center of student anti-war protest. The *Plain Truth* was strenuously anti-communist and did not speak out against the war. Instead, Ted Armstrong's repeated prognostication was that America had won its last war. He quoted God's threat to "break the pride of your power" (Lev. 26:19). In context, it seemed as if God was chastising Israel for having that pride in the first place, instead of trusting in God. But in Ted Armstrong's telling, it was a good thing for a nation to have pride in its power. He often contrasted our country to modern-day Israel, which, he said, still had that pride, as demonstrated in the Six-Day War just three years earlier. Articles in the *Plain Truth* portrayed college protesters much as the silent majority viewed them: unpatriotic, disloyal, and hairy. Yet at the same time, the biblicist theology of the church included a literal understanding of the sixth commandment, "thou shalt not kill," which the church interpreted to mean that military service was forbidden for a Christian. This dove-tailed with its understanding that this was not God's world, but Satan's, and that the end of the age was imminent so that Christians, in general, had no business being involved in it.

I had duly registered for the draft after my eighteenth

birthday, and from then on, obediently carried my draft card in my wallet. Yet the combination of the opposition to the war on campus and my growing inner alignment with the teaching of the church made it clear I could not serve in the military, not even in a non-combatant role far from Vietnam. As long as I remained in college, I was relatively safe with my II-S student deferment but began looking for alternatives. I considered going to Canada. One of my teachers had a brother who taught at McGill University in Montreal; I could transfer there and simply remain after graduation.

With trepidation, I broached the subject with my father during a visit home as we worked side by side, preparing holiday party trays in the delicatessen. Knowing his own experience in Guam and Okinawa, as well as his scorn for peaceniks, I braced for his reaction, but then he surprised me. "I've seen war," he said. "If there were any way I could go in your place so that you wouldn't have to see what I've seen, I would."

After baptism into Worldwide, I learned their legal department could advise me. Their advice: to get my views on record by filling out the paperwork, but not to request a change in status as long as I had the II-S student deferment.

I requested the forms in November and filed them a month later, after laboring over a statement of beliefs, putting it through at least three lengthy drafts as if it were a

college term paper. In addition to numerous Biblical references, I cited Abraham Lincoln's opposition to the Mexi-
can War and Leo Tolstoy on non-violence. As it turned out,
I didn't need much of what I had written, the form only
had space for short answers for the questions posed. As it
was, I added a supplementary sheet to complete two of my
answers. But I left out Tolstoy, which was probably just as
well; after all, he was Russian.

My dad, my former roommate Andy, and John, the
minister who directed my Spokesman's Club, wrote letters
of support to file with the application.

By the time the draft board reclassified me after I left
B.U., I had been accepted to Ambassador College, which
meant I was eligible for the IV-D status for ministers of
religion and divinity students. Even though the college
stressed we should not come with the expectation of becoming ministers, the only major it offered for men at the
time was theology, so technically all of us were in training
to become ministers. This meant I never had to appear before my local draft board to defend my beliefs and never
had to answer the questions of what I would do if someone
were raping my sister, or whether, had I been in Germany in 1933 with foreknowledge of what would happen, I
would have assassinated Hitler.

Toward the end of December, Fred Kellers stopped by.
Gene Hogberg, head of the church's News Bureau in Pasadena, had told him that he and some others were coming

to Boston to cover the annual meeting of the American Association for the Advancement of Science. Hogberg had asked if someone local could take them from the airport to their hotel. Fred thought of me. He advised me to be discrete about my hopes of attending Ambassador, yet he thought that once they learned that I was a photojournalist, they might find more use for me than just one airport pickup. Gene arrived with photographer John Kilburn, cameraman Jim Jensen, and Stig Erlander, the college's chemistry professor. Sure enough, when the group found out, they asked if I would be free to tag along to the meetings. After a day of working with them, they had one more errand in mind. Garner Ted Armstrong would fly in the next day in the Falcon, the church-owned jet that he co-piloted. Would I be willing to drive some of them to the airport to pick him up? Just as had Fred Kellers, they advised discretion. Ted Armstrong did not like being fawned over by the members.

When he arrived, my first impression, after years of listening to him on the radio and reading his articles and books, was negative. It was not only due to his coffee-and-doughnut halitosis and his short stature. It was more instinctive; the thought crossed my mind that I was serving God and not a human. I left that train of thought aside to concentrate on finding my way (traffic to and from Logan Airport was a nightmare back then) and not get distracted by the chatter of the guys joshing and cutting one another.

I spent the next days attending sessions, sometimes with others from the crew, sometimes on my own. My green herring-bone suit jacket got a good workout, as did my camera. One of the highlights: a moon rock on display, brought back just months earlier from the first landing.

It wasn't long before the crew began to ask why I wasn't at Ambassador College; my photojournalism skills would be useful. It was John Kilburn who first brought it up. He was a cheery but no-nonsense ex-Marine. He spoke his mind and often named things that others were thinking but didn't articulate. Gene, by contrast, was quiet, thoughtful. He walked with a limp, which held him back from the sports he would have gladly played while growing up in the Chicago area. I was to spend much time with him in various parts of the world over the next twenty-five years and always thought very highly of him.

I shared my experience in my next speech at the Spokesman's Club. Fred Kellers was the guest director that night and liked my insight of following God, not man.

This interlude was a highlight of my fourth long, dark New England winter. In the three previous, I had shared my living space with roommates, including Andy, with whom I could talk for hours about every imaginable subject, and spent every available moment with Sian.

Now, I spent the evenings when we didn't have a Bible study or a club meeting alone. It was the deepest loneliness I had yet experienced, deprived of companionship and tenderness. I had my tape recorder to keep me company and played many favorite LPs repeatedly. One of the few new ones, *Déja Vu* from Crosby, Stills, Nash, and Young, provided my anthem through the winter: "Rejoice, rejoice, we have no choice but to carry on." Another new one I had taped was Joni Mitchell's third LP, *Ladies of the Canyon*. Some songs reflected her new home in Laurel Canyon, in Southern California, but others had the chill of a northern winter. One of them, "Rainy Night House," was addressed to "a holy man on the FM radio;" the next track described an encounter with "The Priest," whom the narrator encountered in an airport bar. I wondered if she had crossed paths with Ted Armstrong, but dismissed the thought.

The weekly contact with John, the associate pastor, in his capacity as club director in New Hampshire, led to deeper involvement with the church. I fasted regularly that year. The church recommended that each member should fast once a month, but said that more was better if one hoped to be of service to the Work. Fasting was a means of drawing closer to God. By denying our physical needs, the idea was to focus on spiritual needs, to humble ourselves. To pray more earnestly for others and for the needs of the work. One week, I had finished a fast just before leaving for that week's club meeting. That evening, John devoted much of his closing evaluation to the manpower needs of the Work and that we shouldn't let our selfishness stand in the way of serving God. It struck home, and I went up to him afterward and said that if there were any way that I could be useful, I would be happy to.

The answer wasn't long in coming. His wife was experiencing morning sickness in her second pregnancy. If I could spend one or two days a week accompanying him on his visiting rounds, that would relieve her. So, for the next few months, I did that. I would often spend the night on a sofa in his office after club, then spend two days on the road with him, traveling all over Maine, Vermont, New Hampshire, and western Massachusetts.

Within a year of returning to services, now I was the silent, friendly second man. I only spoke when spoken to. Such as by the woman who turned to me after listening to one of John's explanations and asking me what I thought. She seemed amazed when I replied that I saw it exactly as he did. As we drove home late at night, taking turns driving his Plymouth fleet car, with WQXR, the classical music station from New York City, playing on the car radio, we discussed the day's visits. This gave me the chance to ask him about various answers he had given, and his insights into the people we'd visited. In this way, John became a mentor to me.

He cautioned me not to tell anyone that I was accompanying him; it might lead to envy among others in the area. Even worse would be if anyone found out when I arrived at college, if I were accepted, given Herbert Armstrong's dim view of anyone entering to become a minister.

My involvement couldn't help but spread, though. I made a note of the names of those we visited and felt a responsibility to pray for them. Some of them would be invited to services and shared with me how they were doing. Some of them may have mentioned to members that I had been the second man on the visit.

Spending part of each week in New Hampshire cut even further into my commitment to classes. I continued to put more work into my photo class than in the others but struggled in that as well. In the fourth semester, after three semesters working with black-and-white film, we switched to color. We used Ektachrome film, which we developed ourselves. I struggled with exposure, exhausted chemicals, and, most of all, for ideas. We had weekly assignments, but the main project was a slide presentation on a topic of our choosing. As my fourth New England winter waned, I chose the coming of spring. I recorded a track from the Beatles' new LP, *Abbey Road*, "Here Comes the Sun," and brought the tape to use as a soundtrack. When I put the tape on the classroom machine, the song played backward for reasons I don't understand to this day. I became flustered, and the presentation was a fiasco.

At the time, it was embarrassing, and it didn't help my grade for the semester, but in the long run, it was a valuable part of my education. I had learned the value of arriving early and testing all the equipment before a presentation.

Meanwhile, I hadn't heard from the Ambassador admissions committee. Four years earlier, when I had applied to colleges, the acceptances came by mid-spring. Now, graduation approached, so I signed up for job interviews with recruiters who came to SPC. One was with Gannett newspapers, owners of our local daily at home, the Plainfield *Courier-News*.

The interviewer asked me a question about a hot local issue. Rather than admit that I hadn't been following it, I bluffed but sensed I hadn't fooled the interviewer. A second valuable lesson, but one that took me longer to learn, since I always had been quick on my feet, and, at my worst, glib. Eventually, I learned I could admit not knowing something and not have the roof fall on me.

My senior year in Boston ended with a bang and a whimper. The bang was at Kent State when the National Guard had opened fire on demonstrators protesting the Vietnam War, killing four. The B.U. administration immediately canceled the last weeks of classes on our politically active campus, including final exams, and closed the dorms, effectively sending us home. Nor was there a graduation ceremony. Professors had to estimate grades based on course work and participation during the semester. We seniors had no graduation ceremony. I received my diploma in Pasadena a half-year later.

That was the whimper.

With no word from Ambassador, any plans I made were

tentative. I packed my books, clothes, and home-made furniture into a seven-foot U-Haul trailer and moved to New Hampshire. There, just north of Concord, I shared an apartment with another church member, Tony, who had just graduated from the University of New Hampshire. We worked at a variety of jobs, first on a house painting crew, then a couple of weeks' night shift on an assembly line (I no longer remember what passed beneath our hands). Figuring there had to be something better than that, we switched to a chicken plant, cutting frozen chicken for the pieces required by Colonel Sanders. We finished the summer in a factory that made large wooden roof trusses.

It was a crash course in the way many people live. There was an experienced painter, for instance, who stopped for a case of beer on the way home every night and said it was how he got the paint fumes out of his lungs. I also learned things about myself. I surprised both the owner of the paint crew and myself the first time he sent me up a tall ladder to take the shutters off second-story windows; it didn't bother me at all. Other things that summer did. I learned I didn't like switching back and forth between night and day shift. In fact, I hated assembly lines in general, even at the roof truss factory. There were some workers there, power screwdriver in hand, who enjoyed climbing all over the trusses that passed by, but I didn't. Nor did I like the combined noise of the tools and the top-40 radio that played the same few songs over and over all day long. I don't know if I would have liked "Candida" any better had I known it was sung by Tony Orlando, who had responded so enthusiastically to the songs Andy and I demonstrated for him a year earlier. As it was, the song just got on my nerves.

The worst was the chicken plant. I can't remember anyone who enjoyed his role on the three-man crews. One took the frozen chicken out of the crate, took out the guts and passed the chicken to the one standing at the band saw. He cut each into the same prescribed eight pieces, while the third caught the pieces in a plastic bag and put them in a slowly-filling box.

Something else bothered me in addition to assembly lines: I learned that I didn't like to have my quality as a worker defined by whether I clocked in at 7:58 or 8:01. Nor did I enjoy the last few minutes of the shift, when there wasn't enough time to begin a new project, and you waited for the bell to ring so that you could clock out. Those were some of the longest minutes of my life. I understand that if a team has a coordinated task to perform, it lets everyone down to arrive late. In the years since, I've even learned to apply Lombardi time and wait patiently for others. But one of my life-goals became to avoid a job with a time clock.

Social life revolved around the church members and included one of my most romantic memories and one of my most embarrassing. The good one is of a weekend visiting a family in Stowe, Vt., where a widow lived with two sons and a daughter, Cheryl. I arrived on Friday night after work. The next day, we drove to Montreal, my first time in Canada, where a congregation had recently begun; it was closer to Northern Vermont than Concord, N.H., so this family attended there. On Sunday, we visited the Trapp Family Inn, after which Cheryl, who was my age, took me on a hike, including a swim in the clear water of a rock pool teeming with trout.

I would have liked to get to know her better, but there was no time. I finally got an acceptance letter in mid-July, so now I knew that in a month, I would fly to California. And when I mentioned how much I enjoyed the weekend to my mentor, he warned me off. I was going to college, she wasn't.

The other memory also involved the complicated boy-girl relations in such a church. Two girls in the area, Mary and Kathy, fresh out of high school, had taken an apartment not far from the one I shared with Tony, a cramped attic. After they fixed it up, they invited the two of us over. Kathy liked to paint, and when we got there, presented me with a portrait she had painted from a snapshot of me. My reaction was as inappropriate as possible.

Sermons at church repeatedly hammered at the vanity we all allegedly suffered from. I don't know how well they applied to some of the down-trodden, but I felt as if I were constantly wrestling with an out-sized ego. I exploded when I saw the portrait. "Why would I want a portrait of myself?" I exclaimed, with no heed to how hurt Kathy must have been.

And the portrait was well-done. Had I thought calmly for a moment before reacting, I would have realized how much my mother would have liked to have it while I was on the West Coast, far away.

In mid-August, I left my furniture behind in New Hampshire and only took my books, records, stereo, and clothes to New Jersey, where I spent a week visiting my family. I fasted three of my few days with them in preparation for what was to come, while the locusts, who made their cyclic appearance that summer, sang.

Chapter Three

Orientation week culminated in my first full weekend on the campus. A student work crew transformed the gymnasium on Friday afternoon by laying tarp over the hardwood basketball court and setting up hundreds of folding chairs for three weekend services: Friday evening, Saturday morning, and Saturday afternoon. The resulting college chapel offered no pews nor stained-glass windows depicting Bible scenes. Nor was there an organ, bell tower, or cross. This wasn't a deficit. This break with traditional ideas about sacred space was by design.

Normally, the Friday night service was formatted as a Bible study, with the minister who conducted it seated at a desk. That first week's Friday evening event was billed, however, as a preaching service, conducted by Herbert Armstrong. A rostrum stood on the provisional stage placed against the south wall. It was larger than the pulpits of most churches—over-dimensioned, like the hour-long sermons proclaimed from it. Armstrong began by announcing the next afternoon's service. He explained, for the benefit of any entering students not aware of it that "we" observe the Sabbath. With this simple statement, he glided over the ambiguity of just who "we" were (was he referring to the college, or to the church that sponsored it?) while introducing one of his distinctive teachings: the observance of the seventh day. He went on to assure us, however, that no one was required to attend.

Armstrong's topic that evening was the difference between the average college mind and the Ambassador student mind. The phrase reflected his training in advertising: Identify (or invent) a difference between your product and that of your competitors. Were our minds his products? He set the stage for his point by first comparing the human mind and the animal brain. He attributed the difference—the human ability to think creatively, constructively, and to exercise will—to the "spirit in man."

This was a concept that had recently begun to fascinate him, and we were to hear more of it in the coming years. The phrase appears in some Bible passages, such as Job 32:8: "But there is a spirit in man, and the breath of the Almighty gives him understanding." This echoes the creation account in Genesis, where God is said to have breathed the breath of life into the first human, who became a living soul (Gen. 2:7). This transformative agent was not itself the "soul," Armstrong stressed, which according to Ezek. 18:4, can die. Nor could this "breath" or "spirit" of God be equated with the Holy Spirit, which—given the New Testament's emphasis on the Holy Spirit dwelling only in truly converted Christians—could not be in all humans in general. This careful differentiation of terms that are commonly lumped together was one of the features of Armstrong's writings that had attracted me from the start and counteracted my aversion to his overdone typography, with its extravagant use of italics, boldface, underlining, exclamation points and all-capitals.

As a skillful popularizer, Armstrong buttressed his argument by analogy with modern technology, in this case, tape and a tape recorder. The brain was a machine that inscribed sense impressions on the human spirit. The breath of life, this "spirit in man" was the crucial component that differentiates humans from animals. The spirit doesn't see or hear, but all knowledge is recorded on it. This spirit of man "goes upward" after death, as the King James Version renders Eccl. 3:21, which Armstrong understood to mean that this record of each individual's experience and thought is stored in the presence of God—a vast celestial tape library—so that it could assure the continuity between our identity in this life and in the resurrection.

Armstrong's interpretation coincided with research of Robert Kuhn. Kuhn had come to Ambassador two years earlier, aged 24, after completing a Ph. D. at the U. C. L. A. Brain Research Institute. His research led him to conclude, like some brain specialists before him, such as Wilder Penfield and John Eccles, that a non-physical component in the mind was the best explanation for the difference in animal brain and human mind. Kuhn was one of those highly educated people Armstrong liked to boast of attracting to Ambassador.

Armstrong's own approach was not neurological, but theological. His interest was not what made the human mind special, but with what had gone wrong with it. To explain this, he spent a long time talking about Satan. We heard more about Satan in those years than we did about Jesus. Armstrong launched into this with an exposition of Isaiah 14, where Babylon's fallen king is taunted. King Nebuchadnezzar had refused to acknowledge God, therefore, according to Armstrong, Satan was his God. His grounds for saying this came in verse 12, where the subject of the taunt becomes Lucifer. The King James translation retained this Latin word for light-bringer in keeping with a long tradition of understanding it as a name, an alternate way of referring to the devil. As Armstrong read verses 13 and 14, he emphasized the five-fold "I" that reflect Lucifer's ambition and self-exaltation. After expounding this, he had us turn to Ezekiel 28, where, in a manner reminiscent of Isaiah 14, two dimensions appear. After a tirade against the "prince" of Tyre comes a lament over the "king" of Tyre, who was full of wisdom, perfect in beauty, and had been in "Eden, the garden of God" (verses 12–13).

I had my over-sized, wide-margin, leather-bound Oxford Bible open on my lap and had no difficulty turning from passage to passage after completing the college's home study Bible course and more than a year of attending services. I had already marked these passages and would turn to them often during Armstrong's sermons in subsequent years. And the Scofield notes in the Bible my grandmother had given me when I was baptized into Worldwide the year before corroborated much of what Armstrong said.

From a reference to the "workmanship of thy tabrets and thy pipes," Armstrong claimed that this personage was the original author of music. Now that he is perverted, he creates all the perverted music of the day (perverted music, I came to learn, was whatever music Armstrong didn't enjoy listening to). This was an aside, and he didn't explain how Satan "authored" that music, or whether any music existed that was "authored" by humans.

More insight on the college's view of the origin of music came four weeks later from his son Ted, who included the announcement of Jimi Hendrix's death in his sermon. He went on to comment that, although Hendrix sought to hear sounds from out of this world, he never heard celestial music. What he heard instead, Ted Armstrong asserted, but that of terrestrial beings chained to this earth, seeking minds through which they can transmit their tortured creations. Over the next few years, I learned that while Ted

Armstrong's taste in music didn't coincide with that of his father, in condemning what they both called "hard rock," they seemed to agree. It wasn't just not to their liking, it was demonic.

As I sat on both occasions and listened, my own mixed feelings about the music I admired churned in me. From the time I discovered rock 'n' roll at the tail-end of its golden era, in 1959, I had been a fan. Elvis Presley, Fats Domino, Jerry Lee Lewis, Little Richard, Chuck Berry, and above all, Buddy Holly. One of the main sources of their style was church, especially the less-formal kind similar to what I had experienced in our biannual vacations down south to visit my mother's family. So, some of it didn't just seem lewd (not a problem for a teenage boy); worse, a song like "Great Balls of Fire," whose title was a phrase current in Pentecostal circles, seemed sacrilegious. But it rocked, it made you feel good when you listened.

My early ambivalence sharpened as the love and peace of Woodstock faded. The recent fissure of the Beatles left the Rolling Stones as the undisputed premier rock band. The Stones' recent LPs added Satanism to the misogyny that had always been a troubling element in their songs. Yet at Altamount, the anti-Woodstock held the previous December, they seemed as stunned as everyone in the crowd in front of them when one of the Hell's Angels hired for security stabbed a young man who had approached the stage with a gun as they played. This came but a few months after one of their own, Brian Jones, had been found floating face-down in a swimming pool.

It seemed as if there were two paths. One led to drug-induced early death, the other, to sitting at the feet of an infallible apostle who could explain it all from an unassailable source, the Bible. I had chosen the second, which led to me sitting on a folding chair on the last Friday evening in August with open Bible and notebook on my lap.

After decrying perverted music, Armstrong then had us turn to Genesis 1 to, as he expressed it, turn from prehistory to history—thus clearly signaling, without dwelling on the point, that he understood this account as literal and historical. He turned to the creation accounts in Genesis 1–3 in nearly every sermon I heard from him over the next fifteen years; it was central to his understanding, as the next few minutes of his sermon demonstrated. Six days completed the physical creation with the final act being the creation of man. From God's announcement to make man "after our kind," Armstrong deduced that man is not an animal, but made after the God kind, that is, the God species.

With the onset of evening, the seventh day began, the first sabbath; this divine rest signaled the beginning of spiritual creation. God placed the first two humans in a garden with two special trees of symbolic import, the tree of life and the tree of the knowledge of good and evil. "Eating" the fruit of the tree of life, Armstrong commented, was a symbol of receiving the Spirit of God.

The scientific method, Armstrong claimed, began with the decision to eat from the tree of the knowledge of good and evil instead of the tree of life. He termed this "the abrogation of knowledge production." As he characterized it, the first step in science was to reject all revelation and to learn from experience and experiment. God, however, decides what is right and wrong; man's prerogative is to choose whether to obey. Humans obey the physical laws, which brings material progress, culminating recently in putting a man on the moon, but have decided not to obey the spiritual, doing instead what is right in their own eyes, which was, in Armstrong's telling, invariably wrong, evil.

This rapid survey, which hardly left us time to ask ourselves how Armstrong's account of the origin of science in disobedience could nevertheless lead to obeying physical laws, was only the buildup, however, to the culmination: the contrast between the ordinary college mind and the Ambassador student mind. The unspoken assertion was that no students anywhere else sought to do the right thing. An "Ambassador mind" in his telling, was one that accepts revelation. Revelation wasn't limited to the text of the Bible—which would have been problematic enough—but included Armstrong's interpretation. In practice, this meant that if science calls into question Herbert Armstrong's interpretation of the Bible, then it is science that is wrong. If one nevertheless accepts the evidence of science, then that is evidence of a competitive instinct, of self-exaltation.

Thus, Armstrong had laid the groundwork, before classes began, for indoctrination. The manipulation of his argument is clear to me now in retrospect, but at the time, I soaked it up. He excelled in marketing, and together with his personal charisma and air of conviction, he was a persuasive speaker. Here I sat, at last, nearly seven years after hunkering in my basement refuge in the weekend after the Kennedy assassination with copies of the *Plain Truth* I had found around the house and a copy of Bob Dylan's *Freewheelin'*. Now I had arrived in Pasadena, the headquarters of the work that published the magazine and an assortment of booklets. After spending four years at another school, having what Armstrong styled as an average college mind, I was eager to have that mind remolded as the Ambassador student mind.

Armstrong spoke again the next afternoon in what was billed to outsiders as the college chapel service. He picked up on his themes from the previous evening, challenging us with the question of why we were here. Noting that 40% of the incoming class had previously attended another college, he once again raised the uniqueness angle, which he summarized as learning the right way to live. He then declaimed that if we didn't want to learn the right way to live, we might as well pack up and go home. This was masterful practical psychology, indeed, manipulation. Which of us would say within himself, "I don't want to learn the right way to live"?

In the course of his sermon, he told us that he began dreaming of publishing a magazine immediately after his conversion experience, seven years before the first issue of the *Plain Truth* appeared. The time leading up to his conversion had been spent wrestling with two issues, the seventh-day Sabbath and evolution. The lead article in his new magazine was to be about indoctrinating the young about evolution. He commissioned a cartoon to illustrate it, with a teacher holding a large funnel over the heads of her pupils. Ironically, I experienced more indoctrination in Ambassador classes than I ever had in any level of school. Yet even when I began to notice this, I put it down to limitations on the part of the Ambassador teachers, and not an indictment on the entire college's system of instruction.

In a little under three hours, Armstrong had with these two sermons laid the groundwork for the school year. Along the way, he had touched on many of his distinctive teachings, confirming me in my conviction that I had arrived where I could now drink from the fountain of truth.

The messages from that first weekend were supplemented on Tuesday afternoon by the first of the weekly forums, at which a faculty member would address the entire student body. Rod Meredith took this one and outlined four specific personal growth goals we must pursue while enrolled in Ambassador. Many applicants were turned down, he told us, and we who were chosen must excel in developing our minds, bodies, personality, and character. He pointed out that with 550 full-time undergraduate students and over 700 in all, the college was at the limit of its capacity, and cuts could easily be made. (One of the first to go was the boy who sat at the desk next to mine in our dorm. He was simply gone, without explanation). Meredith urged us to discipline ourselves by scheduling our time. He warned us against dating anyone frequently (his term: "heavy dating"). He concluded by reminding us of something we were well aware: Many of our contemporaries were in Vietnam, but we too were engaged in a war—a spiritual war.

Ted Armstrong, who had been at the Big Sandy campus the previous week for orientation, struck a similar note when he conducted services the following weekend, but his point of comparison, surprisingly, was a different group of our contemporaries, the war protesters and hippies. Armstrong told us that we, no less than they, were revolutionaries. And like them, we were not irrelevant, despite being few in number. Lest we get the wrong idea from his comparison, he went off on a tangent—he was no less prone to interjecting asides in his sermons than he was on his radio broadcasts—to say that there would be no bangs on men (by this, he meant hair on the forehead). But even this petty point was underlined by a bigger assertion: a higher forehead was a sign of intelligence (which never prevented him from mocking "egghead" intellectuals).

One week later, Ted Armstrong spoke again and focused on the pernicious effects of entertainment. The repeated contrast held up to us was the youth culture of the baby boom generation. Little was said about the vast mainstream, or as it had come to be known, as the silent majority—especially when applied to Nixon supporters. It was as if, in his eyes, the life of 9-to-5 respectable station-wagon-driving middle-class drones wasn't attractive to us, but the life of shaggy, denim-clad, pot-smoking, war-protesting hippies was. Maybe he was right, although, with our trimmed haircuts, suits, and Samsonite hard-case briefcases, there was little to distinguish us from the mainstream except that we were non-conformists in our beliefs.

Chapter Four

Meanwhile, classes had begun. My aim in orientation week had been to score well enough on language tests to fulfill the language requirement, but I overshot the mark. My scores on college board achievement tests had gained me a dispensation from language classes at Boston University, but Ambassador had different rules and had its own test. I finished the German test in half the allotted time, so I walked into the next room and asked if I could take a shot at the French exam as well; it had begun at the same time as the German. I hoped that I would score well enough on one or the other to skip a language course and have room in my schedule for something else. Despite initial misgivings, the teacher agreed, and I finished that, too.

Later in the week, when it was time to register for courses, I made my way through the folding tables set up in the large open space on the ground floor of Hall of Administration. As I approached the language table, two teachers, both Swiss, were engaged in energetic discussion. When I reached the table, I discovered they were talking about me. My name was on the top of the results list for both tests, with scores that qualified me for a dispensation, but they urged me to take a language course anyway. I didn't ask them for a reason, but assented, and chose third-year German. There were four of us in the class, Paul, Shirley, Connie, and I.

My course load was heavy on Bible and public speaking, supplemented with journalism, physical education, music, and German. Three mornings each week, all incoming students filled the music hall of the Fine Arts building for the required Freshman Bible course. It was called Church History but was really a two-semester survey of the Gospels (in later years renamed Life and Teaching of Jesus to reflect this). In addition to Robertson's *Harmony of the Gospels*, the only required reading for the course was Chapter 15 of Gibbon's *Decline and Fall*, which depicts the rise of Christianity in a way that dovetailed with Worldwide's portrayal of it as a counterfeit of the true church.

We sat in comfortable concert seats as Rod Meredith gave a running commentary on Robertson's *Harmony*. I had my copy open and made notes directly in the margins as he addressed us "fellows and girls." Upper-class students impatiently waited each year for Meredith to cover the wedding feast in Cana (John 2) since many incoming students came from the Bible belt. Prohibition ruled on the campus as each school year began and wasn't lifted until Meredith's description of Jesus turning water to wine.

My markings stop about four-fifths of the way through the book, indicating that's probably as much as he covered that year; he, like the Armstrongs, was prone to go off on tangents. Many of his stories were about his childhood and youth in Joplin, Mo., as a miler and golden-glove boxer. Others recounted his courtship of his wife, née McNair, whose four older brothers had preceded her to Ambassador. The object of his attention also spent time with another guy, so Meredith went on the attack, asking her what she saw in him. "Well, I think he's cute," she replied. "Cute! Cute! If he's cute, you ought to slap him and send him home to his mother," was his retort. The college, in general, had very clear ideas about genuine masculinity and femininity, but it became clear over the year that this was a special interest of Meredith's.

Some of his anecdotes were more closely related to the passage he was expounding. Jesus's teaching on divorce, for instance, brought to mind a minor traffic accident he had with Elizabeth Taylor's car. Anxious to avoid possible lawsuits or publicity, her chauffeur tried to reach a quick agreement with Meredith, offering various inducements in the name of "Miss" Taylor. "Miss!" he exclaimed to us. "She was Mrs. Hutton, then Mrs. Todd, then Mrs. Fisher, then Mrs. Burton." These stories spewed forth with tense energy, then he would push up his plastic eyeglasses with a finger and flash his boyish, almost sheepish grin.

Once, when dealing with a series of accounts in the Gospels of miraculous healings, he seemed to imagine that some of the more zealous of us were formulating the taunting question in our minds of why we didn't see such works today. "Just you wait, Ron Washington (son of one of the few black pastors in Worldwide), just you wait, Henry Sturcke, until we send you out with a vial of anointing oil! Let's see what you can do!" But no, I had not been thinking that. Did his vehemence betray a gnawing question in the back of his own mind?

Given his torrent of rhetoric, it's not surprising that there was little time in class devoted to questions or discussion. Questions that were posed anyway often met with defensive, reflexive answers. I saved my questions for after class when I found him approachable and ready to engage in dialogue.

Meredith remained one of the dominant personalities on campus for most of my time in Pasadena. Given this ample exposure, it's no wonder that his quirks became obvious. After every conference or set of meetings, he said something along the lines of "many who attended commented that it was the best ever." He sprinkled his writing liberally with quotation marks. He wasn't the only one of the church's writers to do this, but the most extreme. He wrote of trying to "catch" each other's mistakes, of trying to enhance our own "image," at the expense of understanding our part on God's human "team." He encouraged us to "work on" ourselves to become "strong" spiritually. I wasn't sure how to understand this. These were obviously not quotations. Were these terms meant ironically? Irony did not seem a major feature of his personality. I concluded the quotation marks might be an additional form of emphasis, on top of those he emulated from the writing of Herbert Armstrong, such as all caps, underlining, and exclamation marks. Or perhaps he had an English teacher in high school who was sensitive to words she considered slang and thus not appropriate for serious discourse.

Meredith's typical sermon contained a heavy dose of making us, his listeners, feel guilty for our spiritual lethargy. He sought to stir us, to infect us with a spirit of urgency, but often the effect was to make us feel not good enough. I came to feel that his sermons were like cod liver oil or some other purgative. It did one good once a year or so, but one wouldn't want to make it a steady diet. In personal interaction, however, his sincerity and bashful smile were winning.

Those of us with previous college experience also joined the sophomores in the same hall for second-year Bible, or "Systematic Theology." More indoctrination, this time from Richard Plache. Tall, brilliant, witty, charismatic, he was also dean of students. One major aim of the course was to make us into good creationists. We read the required text, Whitcomb and Morris's *Genesis Flood*. Our assigned term paper was a refutation of a book promoting evolution. I chose *The Meaning of Evolution* by George Gaylord Simpson, and my research centered on highlighting every instance of the use of the words "presumably," "perhaps," "we may suppose," and other words and phrases I now realize are the sign of a careful scholar. Yet I thought I was refuting the author.

Plache's course was also lecture-based, but in this case, not free-form as with Rod Meredith, but tightly organized with a plethora of points. Exams consisted of regurgitating these points. As drill and rote learning was never my strong suit, my test grades were not high.

The grade on my spring semester term paper helped pull up my final grade. The assignment was to focus on how an institution of our choice would be in the Millennium. I chose newspapers. It was not a surprising choice, given my previous degree. There was also an element of resistance to an anti-intellectual tone on campus, one expression of which was a suspicion of mainstream media. To me, however, the free press served an important function in this world, and I expected it would continue to do so in the world tomorrow.

My ambivalent feelings came out in the paper. At his best, I wrote, a journalist is a public servant, providing citizens with vision, both clear- and far-sighted (I entitled my paper "Where There Is No Vision, the People Perish," a quotation of Prov. 28:16). At the same time, I lamented the adversarial tone of the press toward the government. This, along with susceptibility to pressure from the business side of publishing, was a weakness that would no longer characterize newspapers in a world under divine rule.

After Jesus Christ's return, freed of these pressures, newspapers would flourish as a means to inform, educate, praise, and inspire. Most of all, I wrote, newspapers suffered from neglecting a vital key in interpreting the news: the understanding of prophecy possessed by Worldwide.

Despite being turned in late and featuring my normal quota of typing mistakes struck over, whited out, or corrected by hand, I received an A-.

Another requirement for all freshmen, Principles of Living, met once a week, on Friday afternoon. When Ambassador opened its doors in 1947, Herbert Armstrong was the principal instructor. He taught all the Bible courses, which were the core of the curriculum. Over the years, he delegated most of the courses to others. Principles of Living alone retained his name in the college catalog. Since he had embarked on his world travels, this no longer corresponded to reality. Robert Kuhn took the first class and most of the subsequent ones. He began his first lecture by telling us that while, ostensibly, this course was about sex, in reality, it was about everything. It would cover the nature of man and the purpose of life.

The most obvious reason for mandating this course in the first semester was to meet head-on the challenge of having a coed college where sexual activity was kept under a lid. Not only were we students in the time of life when our hormones raged, but in the society around us, the sexual revolution, or as some of the news magazines called it, the "new morality," was in full swing. Somewhat hysterically, a church publication called this "a greater threat to humanity than the hydrogen bomb." That publication was a book that served as the textbook for the course, *God Speaks Out on the New Morality*, later renamed *The Missing Dimension in Sex*. As with many of Worldwide's publications, it offered a strange combination of socially conservative, even reactionary, teaching, mixed with some profound theological insight.

Some chapters seemed to be based on study papers from those mentioned as co-authors, but in most of the book, the voice is clearly Armstrong's. At the time of writing, 1964, seventeen years after the college opened, Armstrong could boast that the fruit of Ambassador College was radically different than that of the surrounding society, where the divorce rate was one marriage in three and rising. Most Ambassador graduates had married other students or graduates, and at the time, there had been no divorces among them. In the context, Armstrong didn't mention the church's prohibition of remarriage, which might have encouraged more than one mismatched couple to stick it out.

Herman Hoeh guest-lectured once. His articles and

booklets on arcane historical topics had been some of my favorites before I began attending services. After becoming a member, I found he was legendary in Worldwide for his gnomic utterances and other eccentricities. In his lecture, he traced the development of Catholic dogma about sex, drawing heavily on the 1955 book by William Graham Cole, *Sex in Christianity and Psychoanalysis*. This corresponded to a chapter in the book not in Armstrong's writing style; Hoeh likely authored it.

The chapter concedes that the so-called "new morality" was an understandable reaction to the old, which had been based on repression and presented celibacy as superior to marriage. In keeping with the overall Worldwide theological stance, this view was contrasted with one that began with the creation account in Genesis, when God pronounced all that he created, including mankind as male and female, good. Biblical teaching was presented then as one that sanctioned sex, in marriage.

I recall only one class taught by Herbert Armstrong that semester. I had my hardback copy of the book open on my lap, and wrote his comments in the margin as well as in the small, spiral-bound notebook I normally used for note-taking. There were professors at universities back East who lectured from their own books, but they were usually scorned by students. This seemed different to me. One of these marginalia calls up the memory of the excitement of learning directly from him, "sitting at his feet," as the Bible describes the relation of a disciple to his master. I wrote: "Adam and Eve rebelled. All their children have rebelled ever since—but this was not passed on by heredity. To be explained tomorrow." It was the eve of the Day of Atonement, the yearly fast, and I took it for a preview of the sermon he intended to give the next day, but he didn't speak. Still, the note reflects the feeling that "the truth" was continuing to unfold.

Over the semester, it became clear this book was not just any Worldwide publication. Purportedly, it was a sex manual, but an unusual one. For one thing, we were given knowledge we were explicitly told not to use until after graduation and marriage. Beyond that, the book touched on an interlocking set of topics. Taken together, they formed one of the central, distinctive teachings of the church, one that held a unique view of both God and humans.

The book's information about what it calls the "genital system" is prefaced by a quote from 1 Corinthians 12, where the human body is presented as a type of the church. This was not only brought in to correct the belief that these body parts were somehow shameful but also to call attention to what the book called the sacred meaning of sex. Human reproduction was a type of salvation. Here was the key to the importance of the book in the whole structure of the church's teaching. Rather than simply a defense of traditional behavior (don't do it!), there was a connection to one of the church's central teachings, that the purpose of human life was to be reborn into the divine family.

Armstrong argued that the term "born again," as used in American evangelical circles to refer to a conversion experience, was not what the Bible means by spiritual birth. He buttressed this claim by recourse to the use, in the King James version, of the word "beget" in those seemingly-endless Bible genealogies—Abraham begat Isaac and so on. He insisted this "begettal" (a translation of the Greek verb *gennao*), since it was applied to Abraham and the other fathers in those lists, was limited to the moment of conception, and maintained that this narrow meaning applied to the Greek verb as well.

The believer, then, was begotten, not born. Spiritual rebirth occurred in the resurrection. The time we lived between conversion and resurrection was as children of God in embryo. Many churches emphasize this phase of life, commonly referring it to "sanctification," but the unique Worldwide teaching seemed to give it even more importance, with a concomitant stress on character development, even perfectionism.

This doctrine that salvation was divine rebirth was not an esoteric teaching, reserved only for insiders, but one presented in one of Worldwide's most popular booklets, "Why Were You Born?" I had ordered that booklet while still in high school, had read it, but the full meaning of it escaped me. I reread it after my baptism by immersion in 1969 and felt as if I understood it for the first time. Nevertheless, the import and implications of this teaching unfolded more after I arrived in Pasadena. David Jon Hill, a creative and entertaining speaker, gave a sermon early in the school year in which he unfolded the meaning of the teaching, declaring "you will be god as God is god." This meant, he said, ruling over other planets, perhaps becoming incarnate and offering ourselves as expiation for the sins of its inhabitants, something like the Bodhisattva in Buddhist teaching. On the one hand, this took Bible passages that could be understood figuratively and took them extremely literally. On the other, it ignored texts that pointed to the uniqueness of Christ.

This emphasis on spiritual rebirth at the resurrection, after a lifetime of character-development, of overcoming, was directly related to another of Worldwide's distinctive teachings, rejection of the immortality of the soul.

A welcome by-product of this belief was the lack of necessity of a place of eternal torment. If the soul is not inherently immortal, then it's not suffering after death.

Ironically, the Lutheran Missouri Synod, in which I grew up, also officially rejected the view that the soul was inherently immortal, although I never knew it. Here, as in other areas, Armstrong made inroads by being a controversialist. I was not yet fully aware of the gap between what theologians know and what parishioners commonly believe. On this topic, as on many others, Armstrong exploited that gap. My first indication of this discrepancy came shortly after I began reading the *Plain Truth* when I asked my Lutheran pastor about Armstrong's allegation that the common view of hell was an amalgamation of three discrete concepts, aligned with three different Greek words. Pastor Dodge confirmed this was so. When I asked why he didn't teach it, he replied that it wouldn't interest anyone.

Speech training was, next to the Bible courses, one of the mainstays of the college program. It was mandatory each semester for all male students; coeds took one year. There was a weekly lecture, plus "labs," small groups in which we gave our speeches (the coeds were in all-female labs). I was assigned in my first year to a lab section taught by Paul Royer. He was a rigorous instructor, but I throve at first. When it came time for the attack speech, he said that no one would pass who did not convince him that he had attained 90% of his vocal power. I gave it my all, and Royer seemed ready to say I had succeeded, but first asked if any of the class thought I hadn't. My friend Randal Dick was the only one to raise his hand. Royer seemed surprised. Randy, when asked, said, "No, sir, I sit next to Henry in chorale, and he can get much louder than that." Nevertheless, I passed.

We also were all in Ambassador Clubs, the college's version of the Toastmasters-based Spokesman's Club. The irony was that with all that training, public speaking was an area in which I regressed during my three years in college. In the long-run, it all worked out. Sometimes it's helpful to totally dismantle a skill and then rebuild it, but at the time, my self-confidence was badly shaken, which didn't help my speaking.

There were some highlights, though. One was a "get the facts" speech I gave based on Jann Wenner's interviews with John Lennon for *Rolling Stone*, which had recently appeared in book form. Another was an impromptu speech on peace, during which it occurred to me that peace is more than the absence of war. It is the inner peace Jesus promised his followers.

I also took Newspaper Production, taught by Orlin Grabbe. Orlin was David Jon Hill's assistant. Hill, in addition to his other duties as a faculty member and managing editor of *Tomorrow's World* (a third, recently-launched magazine), was the faculty advisor of the student paper, the *Portfolio*.

Along with the nuts and bolts of journalism—the terminology (such as slug, galley, and flat), and the process from reporting and writing an article to its appearance in print—Orlin shared with us the general principles of the school paper, that is, its editorial slant. The *Portfolio* strove to illustrate happiness, respect, and the humor of life at Ambassador, he said. It was to reflect God's Way instead of the "cynical, spiteful, slanted attitude of Satan's system."

Orlin warned against cliché, particularly what he called "the prostitution of foundational precepts of the work." For us to use the phrase "recapture true values," for instance, cheapened the phrase when Herbert Armstrong used it. Orlin made clear from the start that, in addition to providing a historical record of life at the college, it also existed as a training ground for the church's other publications.

We turned in one assignment a week. My first submission came back to me heavily marked with trenchant criticism, but Orlin must have seen potential. As I hoped, I quickly became an exception to the rule that articles by freshmen weren't published; soon my articles began to appear. I continued to write, and toward the end of the first semester, I was told I would become more involved in the production of the paper.

There was also a physical education requirement each semester. The policy frequently changed as to whether we were awarded credit for it, and when we did, whether on a pass/fail basis, or with a grade. In my six semesters, I took swimming, soccer, basketball, weight training, handball, and touch football. The coaching was excellent, but one stood out: Harry Sneider, an unassuming man whom I had for weight training and handball.

Sneider had been born in Latvia in the early days of World War II. While in a displaced persons camp in Germany, he contracted osteomyelitis. His parents refused amputation, his leg was put in a cast, and mended badly. He nearly died. The family immigrated to the U.S. after the war, and Harry developed the ambition to become the world's greatest crippled weight lifter. He came into Worldwide while a college student in Minnesota. Rod Meredith met him on a visit to the local congregation Harry attended and arranged for him to come to Pasadena. He wanted Harry to bulk up the male students so they would look more powerful while speaking.

Sneider refitted the college's rudimentary weight room, and one of his first outside visitors was Arnold Schwarzenegger, newly arrived in the States after winning the title of Mr. Universe. When Bobby Fischer moved to Pasadena after his chess victory in 1972, he asked Harry to train him (Fischer was notable among chess masters for his attention to physical training). This led to press coverage, and Sneider began to be sought out by other athletes such as Dwight Stones, Olympian high jumper. Despite his renown, it impressed me that Sneider treated everyone in the same gentle, respectful, encouraging way, whether a sunken-chested freshman or an Olympian athlete.

Chorale and voice rounded out the program. I had auditioned during orientation week, but didn't expect to be selected for the chorale Although I had sung in children's choir at church, with a solo every Christmas, and had been in the choir in junior high and the boys' glee club in high school, I no longer had a high opinion of my voice for "fine" singing. For the past seven years, I had sung more in folk and rock style. And my fiancée in Boston was a voice major, so I had developed an appreciation for what a good voice was. Instead, my aim was to take the voice lessons the college offered, and the audition was required for those as well. A couple of days later, when a list of incoming students who had been accepted for the chorale was posted, to my surprise, I was on it.

My voice teacher used a method developed by Eugene Feuchtinger, who took ads in *Mad* magazine for his Perfect Voice Institute in Chicago to propagate his theories of "voice personality." I spent hours in front of a mirror, holding the tip of my extended tongue to train the muscles of it to lie flat in my mouth. Each voice student was also assigned an accompanist from among the piano students, but none of them had a free hour at the same time I did for rehearsal, so I was assigned to Don Ecker, a faculty member who accompanied the chorale. In effect, I had two teachers, but profited more from Ecker, who gave me many helpful tips on interpretation.

Chorale became, along with the student newspaper, a major activity of my three years in Pasadena. Rehearsals were late in the afternoon and ran into the start of the dinner hour. I was often exhausted after classes and work, but went anyway, and learned that choral singing is an activity that seems to return more energy than the amount expended. The backbone of our repertoire was sacred and

inspirational songs that had been arranged for Fred War-
ing's Pennsylvanians. Our director, Gary Prather, was one
of the best I ever experienced, on a par with Edgar Wal-
lace in high school and a few others. What stood out in
Prather's case was that with very reduced movements—
I'm sure the audience sometimes saw no hands at all—and
facial gestures, he communicated exactly what he wanted.
Of course, the arms spread wide for a crescendo, but I was
impressed with how much he accomplished with seem-
ingly little.

Helping to bond the chorale as a group was a cam-
pout in the San Bernardino Mountains at a site owned by a
church member on the third weekend of the college year.
That weekend brought my introduction to one of the most
memorable and inspirational figures in Pasadena, Howard
Clark. Clark was one of the miracle stories of the church.
He had been badly wounded in the Korean War, returning
a quadriplegic. He came into the church, and soon after
baptism, he asked Herbert Armstrong's eldest son, Richard
David, for prayer and anointing, and shortly after, left his
wheelchair. The healing was not complete—he lived with
pain the rest of his life—but he had regained his mobility.
He wrote to Veterans' Administration to say he no longer
needed his disability pension, but a look at his medical records convinced the VA that recovery was not possible.

Among other things, his paralysis had robbed him of
his voice. To regain it, he studied every aspect of voice

production and now could fill an arena without a microphone. He had been manager of Worldwide's Photography Department, but his abrasive personality while taking executive portraits (he was no respecter of persons) had led to reassignment as a speech instructor, for which he was also eminently qualified.

Clark spoke to us three times that weekend: Friday evening and Saturday morning and afternoon. I was especially affected by his Saturday afternoon message, "Who and What Is Important?" He suggested that our posturing and striving for recognition might be due to overlooking some of the big things in life. The rest of the message could be filed under "basic Christianity," a topic that meant much to Clark. As far as I could tell, it was something that he not only preached but something he lived, however imperfectly. Some of the more sensitive students never recovered from tongue-lashings he delivered; others were spurred to develop more than they otherwise might have. But he was a man with a big heart whose focus was less on prophecy and doctrine than on brotherly love in action. One time he was assigned to give a sermonette in Pasadena. He stood at the rostrum, read the Sermon on the Mount with no comment, and sat down. Some saw it as a cheap trick or the result of having no time to prepare a message, but others understood the point of the message and felt the sting.

On Saturday night, we had a cookout. In addition to being an accomplished photographer and speaker, Clark was a superior barbecue chef. After feasting on my first taste of buffalo steak, we sang around the campfire. Anyone who wanted could sing a solo number, so I sang a Buffy Sainte-Marie song that meant a lot to me, "Piney Wood Hills." Its lines "I'll return as a pauper, or a king if God wills," resonated deeply with me in light of our millennial expectations.

Chapter Five

In addition to classes, extracurricular activity, social life, and worship services, a big part of campus life was the work-study program. Under this arrangement, every student had a job. When I entered, the hourly wage correlated to one's class (for this calculation, the "first-year" part of my status counted, not the "senior" part). One did not apply for jobs, they were assigned. Although the political leanings of the church leadership were vehemently anti-Communist, this was a system that would have been recognized by any young person in East Germany. Students entered with enough money for first-semester tuition, room, and board. If one lived frugally on what one earned through the work-study program, it was possible to graduate without college debt. The college benefitted from having much of the work done at minimum wage or slightly above. The business manager calculated how much money the church saved if we all declared our objection to Social

Security on religious grounds, and we complied. After all, since Christ's return was imminent, we wouldn't need any retirement funds.

Most incoming students received assignments as gardeners or janitors. We had classier sounding names for these departments, Landscaping and Custodial Services. To land in the Custodial Department, despite having prepared myself for work in the media outreach of the church, was a disappointment, but not a surprise. I had been warned before flying to California that my journalism degree would mean nothing; in fact, it would almost guarantee an assignment to the restroom crew, which turned out to be the case. Regrettably, these tasks were deemed necessary lessons in humility rather than simply acknowledging that such jobs needed to be done.

Of course, Ambassador could have hired a custodial crew, as other colleges did. But how many students at other colleges ever take note of them or feel any appreciation for the work they do? The custodians, the dishwashers, the garbage collectors are often invisible, even when they are standing in plain sight. So, in retrospect, it makes perfect sense that as an incoming student I spent twenty hours a week dressed in my blue custodial uniform, carrying my bucket filled with swab, rags, and cleaning solutions (mixed by the head of the Custodial Department) from dorm to dorm and scrubbed shower stalls, sinks, toilets, and urinals. But at the time, it was, in college-speak, an attitude test. Much of my prayer-closet time that first year was spent trying to wrestle myself into a "good" attitude. Why? Many attested to a job change that seemed to come from nowhere the moment the attitude changed. I wanted to have a good attitude so that I could be transferred, too.

The college did have full-time workers, including custodians, but they trained and supervised us. My supervisor was Willie Edwards. He seemed to understand what he was up against in managing kids like me whose meager experience of life didn't prevent them from imagining that they were cut out for something better. I got badly sunburned during the student beach party at Huntington Beach the day before classes started. When I called in sick, I'm sure he suspected that he had another malingering older freshman on his hands who thought he was too good for this work. But when he showed up in my bedroom under the eaves of Manor del Mar and saw my blistered legs, his attitude quickly changed to one of compassion.

From time to time, I ran into Gene Hogberg, head of the News Bureau, with whom I had gotten along well the previous winter in Boston at the AAAS meetings. It took me a while to get wind of it, but Gene was petitioning the Personnel Department for permission to hire me as well as a couple of other promising new students (one was Mike Johnson from North Carolina, an even better journalist than I, who has remained a lifelong friend). It would have been better if I hadn't gotten wind that something was in the works. The hours bent over porcelain until it gleamed passed even more slowly while wishing I were in the News Bureau instead. As it turned out, filing news clippings is only marginally more interesting than scrubbing tile, but at least I would have something that interested me passing through my hands.

Classes, chorale, club, Bible study, services, and twenty hours of work. That was our week. A couple of months after college began, I learned that my Boston roommate and songwriting partner, Andy, was in California, getting started in a film production career. When he phoned, I was out, and one of my roommates answered. Andy asked him when would be a good time to reach me. The roommate read off my schedule, posted on my bulletin board.

Andy remarked: "If he's still alive at the end of the day, have him call me." When I returned the call, he told me he had met Chad Stuart (of Chad and Jeremy) at a party, who wanted to hear the songs we had written. Andy and I had pitched our songs in New York in the spring of 1969. The response was positive but had never led to anything. With my workload, there was no time to break away to meet up. I doubt anything would have come from pitching them to Chad Stuart, but I'll never know.

Nor did I make any attempt to reconnect with Michael Fennelly, whose band I had been in while in high school. He had hitchhiked to Los Angeles shortly after I left for Boston and became part of the legendary songwriter-collective that recorded as the Millennium. After that group broke up, he fronted a group called Crabby Appleton. Their song "Go Back" had been a success in some markets that summer, but didn't attract much attention in others.

The world of music lured me. Perhaps part of the depth of my commitment to the rigors of Ambassador life was a way of strapping myself to the mast to resist its seductions. Instead of looking up old friends, my social life revolved around others on the campus. After years of hiding my beliefs, I was suddenly among hundreds of other young people who ostensibly believed as I did. Yet there were differences. It was particularly difficult to relate to those who had come to Ambassador from Imperial School, a private K–12 school for children of church members, especially ministers and others who worked at the college. To my mind, it must have been great to have grown up in the church. Children of top ministers, especially the select circle known as evangelists, must have a leg up on their way into the kingdom, I felt. Most of them rebuffed my attempts at friendship. I gradually began to sense that there was resentment in some of them brought on by precisely the naïve notions such as mine projected onto them by those outside. It took me a while to imagine what it must have been like to be dressed-up and led to the front seats at services, where every fidget would be registered by parishioners watching this model family.

An exception became one of my best friends at college,

Randal Dick (the one who could not tell a lie in speech lab after my attack speech). He had spent some years in Imperial. But he had also spent part of his youth in Jerusalem, where his father managed the Church's office. He was one of the most level-headed students I knew. We met while waiting for the college buses to take us to the orientation beach party. He and another student had guitars. I borrowed one and showed him the licks to a song by the Rolling Stones, "Under My Thumb." Six years earlier, the Beatles had debuted in the U.S. and were instantly another sign of the End Times, but now more than one faculty member conceded they had written some good songs. The Rolling Stones, however, were definitely not on the list of Ambassador-approved music, for reasons I understood. But even a song like this one, with its misogynist posturing, was well-played. I sensed Randy shared my love for their musicianship. For the next three years, we sat side-by-side in the tenor section at the late-afternoon, daily rehearsals of the chorale.

In general, I was drawn to others who felt as enthusiastic about the church and its mission as I. One was Jan, a gaunt Dutch youth. He drove himself to get the most out of his college experience, stinting on sleep, spending hours at his desk, fueled by caffeine, in the small office where editorial work for *De echte Wahrheid* (the Dutch edition of the *Plain Truth*) was done. I met him through Denise, a lively, talkative girl from North Carolina whose dark looks

88

proudly displayed her Cherokee heritage. Another of her friends was Chris, a lanky youth from Florida. His dark-framed glasses and slim face gave him the look of sharp intelligence.

In my first fall semester, I probably spent more time with Jan than with any other student. In addition to our long discussions, we often met in the late afternoon, before I had chorale practice, to run a mile on the college track. We didn't mind that this also brought us into informal contact with Rod Meredith, who, while in high school, had set a record as a miler. We didn't go out of our way to court Meredith, but we could sense that anyone who ran track in his free time had a high mark in his book. My friendship with Jan was interrupted when he was transferred to the college's Bricket Wood campus in England at the end of the semester. I went with Denise, Chris, and Vicki, another good friend of Jan's, to the airport to see him off. In the spring semester, Chris and I filled the role that Jan had in each of our lives for each other. Then Chris, too, was gone—off to study archaeology at Hebrew University.

Not all of my new friends were male. In addition to Denise, there were many other girls. Half of the student body, in fact. I imagine a lost, isolated French legionnaire must have felt like this when, after wandering through the desert, at last, a shimmer turned out not to be a mirage but an oasis. I was thirsty for companionship. But there were rules. One of them was a relic of the early days of the college when some of the new students were socially awkward, like the Johnson Boys of an old folk song. To combat this, students were encouraged to date. At least twice a weekend, in fact (escorting a coed to Friday night Bible Study or Saturday Sabbath services was considered a date). At the same time, we were told to date widely. This rule was intended to guard against the opposite danger, romantic involvement. Even necking could be grounds for dismissal.

But the lack of affection didn't mean a lack of emotional involvement. In Pasadena, there were hundreds of women to meet. With some, the chemistry wasn't right, or we got off on the wrong foot with each other, but for the most part, getting to know them was a highlight of my three years there. I became emotionally involved repeatedly, and at least once was head over heels in love. For better or for worse, that was unreciprocated. Of course, it went both ways. There were a few who liked me in a special way, but I was happy just to have them as friends.

Six weeks after classes began, the entire student body boarded buses to attend the Feast of Tabernacles. We were assigned to Squaw Valley, site of the 1960 Winter Olympics. On the way, we stopped in Yosemite. After the warmth and smog of Southern California, this was a welcome change. We stayed in a camp with rustic two-person cabins, hiked and cycled through the sequoia groves and meadows in the crisp air. The vistas of Half Dome, El Capitan, Bridal Veil Falls, both by day and by moonlit evening, seemed to speak of God's grandeur. Our stay lasted only a day-and-a-half, but the experience was so intense I felt we were there longer.

Fortified and inspired, we continued to Squaw Valley, where we stayed in dorms built ten years earlier for the athletes. We spent two days setting up thousands of folding chairs in Blyth Arena so that all would be ready for the opening evening service. Most of our time went into morning and afternoon services on each of the eight days, but some of us fit in a hike during one of the lunch breaks. I remember sitting on a hillside and serenading Margie, one of the coeds who was beginning to be special to me, singing Leonard Cohen's "Sisters of Mercy" and other songs we both liked.

The chorale sang in many of the services, and there were rehearsals on the two evenings before the fun show. The chorale sang at the dance on the following evening as well, so that we had only one free evening. I didn't mind, though; I was in high spirits. One unforgettable highlight was standing on stage, on the north side of the arena, facing the open end with its view of the Sierra Nevada mountains as we sang Sibelius's "Onward Ye People."

It helped that the schedule included many of the best speakers in the church. The prospect of addressing the largest congregation of the year, combined with knowing that theirs was but one of seventeen sermons, spurred them to bring their best. David Jon Hill, in his opening night message, demonstrated not only his gift for bringing scriptures to life but also his ability to make mind-numbing statistics understandable. He expounded Matthew 24, which, with its predictions of wars and rumors of war, was a frequently cited passage in Worldwide sermons. But Hill made it fresh. When he came to famine, for instance, he said that more people on earth had died of starvation that day than were present that evening. One-quarter of a million more would die during the upcoming week while we would live here affluently. The prophecy of earthquakes seemed up-to-date; as many lives were recently lost in five minutes in Peru as would keep the Feast worldwide, he pointed out. Hill set a high standard with this opening message, but many of the sermons that followed throughout the week were equally stirring.

As exhilarating as the Feast was, by the end of the week, the onset of satiety made us ready to return to Pasadena and resume classes.

I hadn't brought a guitar with me when I flew west. A few months into my first year at Ambassador, my parents sent me an unexpected check for thirty dollars and told me to spend it on something for myself. By that time, I had learned that one didn't have to tithe on gifts, which was good, because I was in a third tithe year, that would have taken nine dollars from it. On the same day that I received the check, a classmate showed me his guitar and said he was thinking of selling it. It was a Framus, made in Bavaria, with a slotted tuning head, designed for nylon strings like a Spanish guitar, and a gracefully curved back. I tried it out, and it had a nice sound. I asked him how much he was asking, he answered thirty dollars. The coincidence was too strong, so I once again owned a guitar.

I had sold my nicest guitar, a Guild electric that I had bought from a high school classmate five years earlier, during the summer of 1969, soon after baptism. Herbert Armstrong had sent a co-worker letter begging for special contributions to the building fund for college campus construction. I sold the guitar for seventy-five dollars, the same price I had paid for it, and sent the money as an offering to Pasadena. The fellow who bought it also took up with Susan, the girl I had begun dating after Sian and I split, while I was at Woodstock. He got my girl and my guitar. But now I had a guitar that I treasured for many years until passing it on to our youngest son.

I had also left my record collection behind in New Jersey. Many of the LPs went to my brother Ken, especially those that didn't meet the approval of the church, such as the Rolling Stones, the Pretty Things, and the Village Fugs. The rest went into the basement room in my parents' home, where I had spent many hours listening to them in high school. I did bring my wooden-cased Wollensak 3M tape recorder with its two detachable wing speakers. I had copied some of my favorite LPs onto reel-to-reel tapes, usually three per side, for example, Simon & Garfunkel's *Bridge Over Troubled Water*, a collection Spanky & Our Gang's hits, Judy Collins, and Joni Mitchell. I listened through headphones so as not to disturb the others in our study area. Not knowing how they would be accepted, I didn't bring too many Beatles or Bob Dylan recordings. I did have *Self Portrait* on tape, the strange two-LP collection, mostly covers of songs by others that Dylan had issued that summer.

One of the few LPs I bought in my Pasadena years was a new Dylan LP that appeared soon after I arrived in Pasadena, entitled *New Morning*. I bought it with reduced expectations. The overall tone seemed to be a paean to domestic contentment, a retreat from the culture wars of the Sixties. In a way, a counterpart to my displacement to Southern California. The enigmatic final tracks, "Three Angels" and "Father of Night," added a religious dimension to the whole. But apart from the difficulty of discerning their message, it was not clear what they meant for the entire LP. Was this a component of the domestic bliss he was trying to convey, or did it signal the next direction on his snake-like track, much as "Restless Farewell" had been on *The Times They Are a-Changin'* or "I'll Be Your Baby Tonight" on *John Wesley Harding*?

Since the church didn't celebrate Christmas, birthdays, or other holidays it considered pagan, and since the holy days it did observe were filled with services, Thanksgiving was the one day in the year that could be celebrated in something like the way that most Americans celebrated holidays.

Ione Wade, secretary in the Dean of Students' office, always invited a group of students in addition to local member friends to her home. I was among those invited for my first Thanksgiving there. I took my guitar and provided entertainment, and was invited every Thanksgiving after that. On one of the subsequent years, Lee Pettijohn, an engineer in the television department, was there as well. Before joining the church, he had been an aspiring Nashville cat, and he generously taught me a few licks as we played for the other guests.

Nor did Worldwide observe New Year's Day, but the location of the college along the route of the Rose Bowl Parade was prime territory. We put up stands, rented parking space, and sold concessions and programs. Student labor made much of this possible, and much of the money earned went into our college activity fund, which sponsored, among other things, the senior trip in the spring. Up to a million people lined the parade route each year.

My assignment the first year was an overnight shift at one of the parking lots. It entailed long hours of solitude, not as interesting as pulling an all-nighter on the school newspaper. I had a book with me that I tried to read under a streetlamp, but that strained my eyes, and I put it away.

The Rose Parade was one highlight of the semester break. Another was the church's annual ministerial conference, when regional directors from the international areas, administrators from the sister campuses in England and Texas, district superintendents, other evangelists, and a few other selected ministers came for a week of meetings. One of those that year was John, my mentor from New England. He had attended college in Bricket Wood, so this was his first visit to Pasadena.

A tradition during the conference each year was a formal dance, with the chorale providing entertainment. Gary Prather included numbers to reflect the international scope of the church's activities and tapped my gift for accents by having me sing "Tie Me Kangaroo Down, Sport." Wayne Cole, regional director for Australia, sought me out after we performed. He was understandably curious why there was an Australian he didn't know about in college. It was the first time we met and talked, but it would not be the last.

Chapter Six

Not long after the second semester started, on a Sabbath in February, a fully-packed gym was subjected to an emotional outburst that waxed to a harangue. Garner Ted Armstrong was highly-strung by default but now the string was so tightly wound it risked snapping. Two things set him off this week. One was a manila transmittal envelope sent from the registrar's office with a note saying they were running out of file space so were shredding old college applications and thought he would like to keep the photo from his brother's application.

Richard David Armstrong had been one of the four pioneer students when Ambassador opened in 1947 and one of the first graduates. He was ordained an evangelist, the highest rank in the ministry below Herbert Armstrong. It was he who anointed wheelchair-bound Howard Clark. Shortly after that, Dick Armstrong was on a baptizing tour with another minister at the wheel. As they sped up the Pacific Coast Highway near San Luis Obisbo, their car, which was in the wrong lane, crashed into an oncoming car. The other minister, who had been at the wheel, escaped with minor injuries, but Dick Armstrong sustained multiple injuries and went into shock. He lingered for a week but died after an overnight transport to the U.C.L.A. medical center. He had been transferred because his kidneys were failing, but suffered cardiac arrest before he could be hooked up to a machine. The incident was traumatic for the entire church at the time, but especially so for the family.

Ted Armstrong was in the midst of an evangelistic campaign in Springfield, Mo., and did not see his brother, who was only sixteen months older than he, before he died. Now he held the photo in his hands, still attached to the clipped corner of the now-shredded application. It had been twelve years since the trauma, but clearly, he still felt it. Yet he generalized, accusing all of us of not cherishing the history of the Work, that is, the ministry headed by Herbert Armstrong. He felt this was the most important activity on earth at the time, and an innocuous act such as shredding twenty-five-year-old college applications showed a failure to understand this.

Then Ted Armstrong switched to his second complaint. From the way he treated it, it was equally grievous. The previous week, the faculty basketball team had lost a game to the seniors. Basketball was the main sport on campus, ahead of the second favorite, track and field, but the college did not play against other schools—the program was strictly intramural. Whether student or faculty, you either played, or you were in the stands. Even Dr. Hoeh complied, albeit with his head bent over a book as he sat a few rows up. That year's senior class featured three starters over 6'5", led by former All-American Ray Kosanke. Ted Armstrong was a talented guard, but it's a challenge to have nearly a foot of height disadvantage. Nevertheless, the faculty always won. Except for the previous week, when the seniors surged in the closing minutes, forcing turnovers and otherwise taking advantage of every faculty mistake. One of the few places Ted Armstrong came as close as he ever did to relaxing was in the faculty locker room after a game with a well-stocked beer cooler. Of course, I had no access to that inner sanctum, but I can imagine that the mood after this game was not like that after other games.

The importance of the intramural sports program was underlined by the fact that we had a second student publication to cover them, the *Sportfolio*. Bob Gerringer, the sports editor, came up with what seemed to all the staff as a catchy title to describe the game: "Faculty Snatches Defeat Out of the Jaws of Victory." What none of us considered was that the faculty team might not see the humor in it. We were about to find out otherwise. The starting guard for the faculty team now had the microphone, was dressed impeccably in suit and tie, and was number two in the rank-conscious church, meaning that he was, in our eyes, the second most important person on earth. After accusing the entire congregation of disrespect for the history of the work, he turned his ire on the school newspaper and those few of us who made up its staff.

We were somber at supper in the dining hall that night, but we knew what we had to do. On Monday night, before putting the new edition of our weekly *Portfolio* to bed, we would put out a replacement of the *Sportfolio*, which we called our sackcloth-and-ashes edition. Bob Gerringer left once that was accomplished, then I stayed on and worked through the night to finish the *Portfolio* with the editor, Bob Millman, a student from England who could do a perfect Churchill imitation. We worked back to back at desk cubicles in the Editorial Department on the third floor of the Hall of Administration. At 5 A.M. I got up from my desk to stretch, and walked to a large plate glass window to look at a beautiful full moon in the west, shining onto the deodar cedars on the lawns of the peaceful campus. I briefly soaked in the sight to gather strength for the final push, then returned to my work station, with its large IBM electric typewriter.

I continued typing for another hour. The powerful typewriter made the metal work station rock gently, a pleasant rhythm as I worked. At 6 A.M. I took my fingers from the keys to rest my hands and eyes briefly. Then I noticed that the work station continued rocking, even though I was not typing. When I stood up, I felt the floor shifting. I gingerly sidled in Bob's direction. He had stood as well and was headed toward me. We met halfway between our workstations and clasped each other by the biceps. Locked together in this way, we moved sideways to the nearest door and stood on the balcony that overlooked the entrance level of the Hall. As we watched the chandeliers sway, I broke our silence: "Well, there's one consolation, Bob."

"What's that?" he answered.

"We were doing the Work."

Shortly after that, the words became briefly famous, although in a slightly altered form. Bob went down to the security office in the southeast corner of the first floor. The guard on duty thought he was alone in the building and asked Bob if he had been there, too. Bob struck his full Churchillian posture and declaimed, "If I'm going to go, I'm going to go doing the Work!" This made the rounds, and next Sabbath was quoted by Ted Armstrong in his sermon (the earthquake had struck on his forty-first birthday). Apparently, we had redeemed ourselves.

Some events change the way you look at life in an enduring way. Until then, I had lived with the unexamined assumption (on land at least) that whenever I lifted my foot, the ground would be there to meet it when I set it back down again. I never realized what a basic sense of security this offered. Nor was I the only one affected. One of the dorms had a problem with the disappearance of personal belongings. Soon after the earthquake, every missing item reappeared, exactly where it was last seen.

Life on campus was shaken again a few weeks later, in mid-March, but in a different way. Every Thursday afternoon, we had a forum, a required assembly for all the students. It was often a third weekly sermon, in addition to Bible study and Sabbath services, but focused more on the shortcomings of the students, rather than the wider church. Since the targeted audience was smaller, only half the gym was set up with seating for it. The speaker was invariably a member of the faculty or administration.

This week Richard Plache, dean of students, bestrode the stage, placed himself behind the over-sized rostrum, and spoke not of some infraction of the rules, but on a general lack of love and appreciation for one another. He was an effective speaker, one who knew how to combine intellectual rigor with emotional appeal, and this time, he pulled out all the stops. When he finished, we rose from our seats and milled about, hugging one another and telling each other we loved them. I'll admit that the hugs of some of the coeds were particularly welcome.

For all those who were there that afternoon, as well as some who were not, this went down in Ambassador lore as the love-in. I believe Plache correctly sensed that our emphasis on doing the right thing, obeying all the rules, both those in the Bible and those in the college handbook, had distorted the true spirit of Christianity. Nor should the tension of living in a coeducational setting in which even necking was grounds for dismissal be discounted; there was an element of release in the outburst. But what Plache aimed to achieve was nothing short of a revival. Ted Armstrong was out of town that week, having flown to New York for radio interviews. According to Plache, Ted Armstrong was suffering from strain. Plache's remedy was for the students to assure him of their love and support. Two busloads of students waited at Burbank airport on Friday evening to meet the Falcon when it touched down. However correct Plache's diagnosis may have been, the prescription was no help.

I wasn't among those at the airport, but was on the road bright and early the next morning with Richard Plache and his wife, Ruth. Headquarters ministers often spoke in surrounding church areas, and Plache had an assignment in Norwalk. My Sabbath date was one of the students who played piano. Often, they went to the outlying churches as well to gain experience in accompanying hymns. She asked if I'd like to come. Plache's sermon covered much the same ground as the forum, and he talked enthusiastically in the car for the drive both down and back. As he saw it, Worldwide had fulfilled a first important step by restoring sound Biblical teaching (although his view on the soundness of some of the teachings later changed). But now, in preparation for Christ's return, the second step was to restore what had often been missing: love. Less than four years earlier, I recalled, after my first Worldwide service, my then-fiancée and I had blurted out to the local pastor, "where is the love?"

We returned to Pasadena. Ruth Plache went home to spend time with their children. Afternoon services had begun by the time we reached the college gym, so Richard Plache, my date and I entered as quietly and as inconspicuously as possible. The sermonette had already finished; Ted Armstrong was just beginning his sermon. It soon became clear what his topic would be. The previous evening's show of support at Burbank airport had not pleased him. After spending most of the week in New York City, he wanted nothing more than to hurry home, where one of his children was sick. But that was not all that bothered him. He had been informed of what had happened on campus in his absence. Without talking to Plache about it, he had formed his opinion and spent the sermon time admonishing us to control our emotions. I had the sensation of the very tall man in the seat next to me shrinking. After the *Sportfolio* sermon six weeks previously, I could sympathize.

We were abashed but not beaten. The hope remained that once he was more fully informed, Ted Armstrong would view what had happened in a more positive light. Meanwhile, it was time for chorale members to pack. We were to travel to Big Sandy by bus to combine with that campus's chorale and present a concert accompanied by the Dallas Symphony Orchestra. For those of us too dense to have gotten Ted Armstrong's point, we viewed it as a chance to carry the message of love to our sister campus.

This was my first trip through the Southwest of the U.S. We stopped and ate our sack lunches on the banks of the Colorado River, then made two overnight stops. The first was in Wilcox, Ariz., my first experience of a Motel Six. The second overnight was in Midland, Tex., where Larry Salyer, the local pastor, organized a backyard cookout. We might have enjoyed it more had many of us not begun exhibiting symptoms of Montezuma's revenge from our lunch stop that day in El Paso, but Salyer, with his enthusiasm, made a positive impression. I didn't know it then, but we would work closely together in coming years.

Our bus pulled into Big Sandy, and over the next few days, we experienced a different flavor of the Ambassador experience, more relaxed than in Pasadena. Perhaps the rural setting had something to do with it. When my date for Friday night Bible study remarked how clear the sky was, I replied that there were so many stars blocking the view, I could hardly see the sky. Another of the coeds invited me to go riding with her, an amenity not available in Pasadena. It was my first time in a saddle other than on a pony led by a tether. But with some good instruction and a placid horse, here I was, riding across the fields of East Texas.

Another coed came up to me in the dining hall and

loudly announced she had to meet me because she couldn't believe someone was really named Henry Turkey. She had misheard. I, in turn, found it hard to believe that Mr. and Mrs. Thatcher would really name a daughter Becky.

The Big Sandy campus had opened in 1964, less than seven years before our visit. The campus, built on land donated by the Hammer family (Ted Armstrong's in-laws), was first used as a Feast site. Many of the students lived in Booth City, a collection of two-person booths spread among a scrub pine hillside originally built to house church members for the Feast of Tabernacles. I, however, was quartered in one of the newly-built dorms.

Much of our time was spent in rehearsing the popular opera choruses we would sing in concert. Our first combined performance was in services on Saturday afternoon. That evening, our teamwork was further promoted by a hayride and campfire. Somehow, our resolve to share the spark of the revival was forgotten amidst all the new impressions.

Bob Millman, the *Portfolio* editor, came along on the trip to meet with John Robinson, the Big Sandy journalism instructor. When I entered Ambassador, the format of the *Portfolio*, that is, its page size, was dictated by the need to use the same equipment that the press used for other publications. Now Robinson was planning to switch the layout of the Big Sandy *Portfolio* from tabloid to full newspaper size and adopt camera-ready production.

Bob arranged for me to stay behind for a day to become acquainted with it as well; since he would be graduating in June, it would be good if someone was exposed to this who would continue to work on the *Portfolio* staff in the fall. He also arranged for us to fly back from Dallas, which meant we would return no later than the bus. I was not sorry about missing the bus trip back. While my first experience of Arizona, New Mexico, and the broad expanse of Texas had been interesting, I had no need for another lunch in El Paso.

Chapter Seven

Summer break, 1971, approached, and students began making plans. Seventy-eight students from the three campuses would fly to Jerusalem to participate in the archaeological excavation at the Temple Mount.

Prophecy buffs had long held that the Messiah would return to a temple. The last one (Herod's) had been destroyed by Roman legions nineteen centuries earlier. That's why it was significant that, as a result of the Six-Day War in 1967, the nation of Israel now had possession of the Old City, where Herod's Temple had stood.

The timing of Israel's regaining possession of the Temple Mount seemed especially important to Worldwide, with its calculation that Jesus would return to usher in the Millennium in the fall of 1975, a little more than eight years in the future. This was what had spurred me to request a visit from a "college representative" so that I could begin attending services in the summer of 1967.

108

Despite the significance and Armstrong's claims to have the key to unlock Bible prophecy, the takeover of the Old City took him by surprise. He had announced in a letter to supporters in spring 1967, before the Six-Day War, that the church had contracted with Jordanian Radio Jerusalem to broadcast the *World Tomorrow*, beginning June 7, 1967. In preparation, the church rented a house near Jerusalem for combined office and living quarters for the office manager, Ray Dick (whose son would become a good friend at Ambassador), who would handle the mail generated by the broadcast. When the station went off the air due to the Israeli takeover, the contract was voided. The Dick family moved there nevertheless, despite the cancellation.

With no broadcast, there was no mail for Ray Dick to answer, so he searched for ways to use his time profitably. One way was to volunteer on the Temple Mount dig for a few days during the first season, 1968. Leading Israeli archaeologist Benjamin Mazar lost no time after Israel gained control of the Old City in organizing this project.

Ambassador did not yet have an archaeology department but hoped to develop one as part of its quest for accreditation. Having students dig in Israel seemed like a good step. The first plan was to have its own excavation, under Mazar's supervision, from his list of promising sites. When Ray Dick learned that Mazar was having trouble lining up donors to continue the Temple Mount project, however, he suggested Ambassador invest money in that project rather than in its own dig and have our students volunteer there.

Summer 1971 marked the third time that a contingent of Ambassador students, who made up well over a third of the two hundred total volunteers, participated in the dig. Thirty-two other Pasadena students served as counselors, activity teachers, and workers at the church-sponsored summer camp in Orr, Minn. For the past two years, the college had also sent a few students to Japan to study the culture and learn the language and did so again this summer.

Our gang of four in German III, Connie, Shirley, Paul, and I, had pestered our teacher throughout the school year with questions about a possible future in the Work in Germany. He tried to dampen our enthusiasm by telling us the work in Europe was as big as it was going to get. We were stubborn though and decided to take matters in our own hands. Together with some German II students, we began to talk about going to Germany for the summer to improve our language skills. One of the group, Jon, took a bus to downtown Los Angeles, where a newsstand carried international newspapers, and bought the Sunday edition of *Die Welt.* Jon, Paul, and others perused it and found a want ad for a construction firm in Bad Oeynhausen. This town was near Bielefeld and Hannover, an area purported to have a neutral form of high German. One of us, I'm no longer sure if it was Jon or Paul, responded to the ad, explaining none of us had the necessary qualifications, but that we were interested in summer work. The company passed the letter to the Bad Oeynhausen newspaper, which ran an article about our interest. Various businesses responded with part-time job offers, so we began organizing a summer program. In the end, four students went: Paul, Jon, Rita, and Janet.

Although I had been one of the initiators of the plan, I didn't go. I was sidetracked by something John Kilburn, the photographer I had first met at the AAAS meetings in Boston, cooked up. Frank Schnee, manager of Worldwide's work in Germany, suggested a student could do an internship with the Hennigs, news photographers in Bonn. King Leopold of Belgium spotted the 1969 college yearbook, the *Envoy*, in the Hennigs' office and wanted to meet the man behind such a college. This was one of the factors that led to opening the door to the world trips Herbert Armstrong was now taking.

John thought of me for the internship.

In the end, none of this happened. I had a knack for sticking my nose into things and stirring up interest but held back when it came time to commit. So, while others flew off to Europe, Israel, and the Far East, I had nothing to look forward to but a summer spent cleaning restrooms.

My parents sent me a plane ticket so that I could begin the summer with a brief visit home. I flew east with my classmate, Denise, and Ione Wade, the Dean of Students' secretary. They spent the night at my parents' home before I took them to Kennedy Airport. Mrs. Wade took part in the dig that year, and Denise wanted to see off Chris, whom she eventually married, on his way to study archaeology at Hebrew University as a preparation to teach it at Ambassador when the college added that subject. We reached the airport just as the connecting flight bringing the Big Sandy contingent of diggers arrived.

The brief stay in Westfield gave me the chance to catch up with my sister, Edith, and my brother, Ken. They had both graduated from junior college, and now Ken was engaged and would soon marry. Our dad thought he was too young to take such a step since Ken was twenty, and Ellen, his intended, was nineteen. He asked me to try to talk Ken out of it. I didn't. After spending time with my brother and Ellen, I told my dad I thought they'd be all right. The words of the apostle Paul that it was better to marry than to burn (1 Cor. 7:9) were no doubt in my mind.

While home, I reconnected with two high school classmates, Alan, drummer in our band, and Carolyn, the girl our band leader Mike had left behind when he hitchhiked to California to begin his music career. I also traveled into Manhattan to visit my college roommate, Andy, and his wife Karla in their Upper East Side apartment. Karla worked as a publicist for Bantam Books, and Andy was starting his career as a film producer. Andy and I could always talk for hours, and he shared with me some of his newest music discoveries. At Ambassador, I hadn't been keeping up with the latest, so it was my first introduction to Badfinger. Nor had I been aware that Peter Simon's sister Carly had released her first solo LP. Andy played me the hit track, "The Way I Always Heard It Would Be."

In my three weekends on the East Coast, I visited three congregations. One Sabbath I attended locally, in Union, another found me in the Poconos, where a small congregation met in the administration building of the church's feast site, and a third in Concord, N. H. Shortly before services began there, Jim, who had been Spokesman's Club president when I was part of it, approached me. He was to lead songs that day and told me that my mentor, John, wanted me to give the opening prayer. I panicked—I had never prayed in public before. Without thinking, I blurted out that I would rather lead songs. Jim received approval for the change in duties. It was the first time I led songs in worship services, but at least I had practice. The public speaking course at Ambassador included instruction in song leading, and men took turns practicing their skills in the student center as we gathered near a piano to sing hymns after Sabbath brunch.

My visit to New Hampshire coincided with Gerald Waterhouse's visit. Waterhouse was an evangelist, a Texan with more than a passing facial resemblance to Lyndon Johnson, although without LBJ's height. He was recently divorced when he came into contact with the church, which meant, according to Worldwide's teaching, that he could not remarry. He had aimed to become a professional golfer but entered Ambassador College instead. After graduating, he was sent to England when Dick Armstrong returned to Pasadena, then from there, sent to start up overseas operations in Australia, the Philippines, and South Africa. The lack of a family to consider meant that these pioneer assignments were easier to arrange. Now he went on tours visiting congregations all over the world.

Waterhouse's lengthy messages centered on the world tomorrow, our jargon for the time after the return of Jesus Christ to earth to usher in the Millennium. His take-off point was a book jointly authored by Herbert and Ted Armstrong, *The Wonderful World Tomorrow—What Will It Be Like?* It depicted the Millennium as a time when the earth would be restored and flourish, benefiting from the joys of direct divine rule. This world would not be ruled by Jesus alone, however. The twelve disciples had asked Jesus what their lot would be in the Kingdom, and Jesus promised them twelve thrones, reigning over the tribes of Israel, now regathered and aware of their identity as the leading nations on earth.

Building on this, Waterhouse assigned roles to all the heroes of the Old Testament. Joseph, who had built storehouses for Egypt's grain, would be in charge of the global economy, Daniel, with his experience in the court of Babylon, would oversee all the Gentile nations, assisted by Paul, the apostle to the Gentiles. (It's symptomatic of the overall Worldwide approach to the Bible that the New Testament figure would be subordinate to one from the Old.) But even we members would have responsibilities. Thus, the church's emphasis on developing character. We, the poor and base of the world, the small, faithful remnant in the first resurrection, would be governing directly under Christ. Well, not directly, although the Armstrongs would be very high up in the chain of command. But we were all called to be kings and priests.

This tied in with a second of Waterhouse's emphases: the Place of Safety. The Book of Revelation talks, in 12:13–14, of the saints being hidden during the Great Tribulation. Some fundamentalists see this as a reference to a heavenly rapture.

Years earlier, Loma Armstrong, Herbert's wife, had seen an article in *National Geographic* about the ancient city of Petra in the Jordanian desert. Learning that the name meant "rock" and that these buildings had been hewn out of the rose-colored cliffs, she concluded the place of safety would be on earth, which made sense since the Kingdom of God would begin with the return of Jesus to earth, not in heaven. Once one began looking, one found many esoteric references to this throughout the Bible.

Waterhouse was a fervent proponent of this teaching. His characteristic twist, in line with the picture he painted of the world tomorrow, was that the time in the Place of Safety—three-and-a-half years—would not be wasted; Petra would be a place of final training.

Since both Waterhouse and I were staying in my mentor's home, I not only attended Waterhouse's Bible study but also shared supper with him and John's family. He was only slightly less enthusiastic in a small setting. He aimed to get members focused on what he called the big picture, his way of referring to our calling. For those who bought into this vision, his visits were like mass hypnosis.

After three weeks on the East Coast, I returned west. My flight allowed me to make a layover stop at no extra cost, so I landed in Denver to see my cousin Louise, who had gone there after graduating from college with plans to enter med school, although her studies soon took a back seat to her interest in the outdoors. In my short time with her, she gave me a taste of the old West by taking me to the nearby deserted mining town of Black Hawk, then driving to Estes Park, where I experienced a summer thunderstorm with snow for the only time of my life. Knowing me as well as she did, she also organized the perfect wake-up the next morning. She had slipped into the kitchen, put on coffee, and scrambled eggs, then she put the fourth side of Bob Dylan's *Blonde on Blonde* on the turntable so that I slowly drifted into consciousness to the call of "Sad-Eyed Lady of the Lowlands".

I returned to California, resigned to cleaning restrooms, and resolved to do the best job I could. I began with a fast to have the right attitude. Unlike previous fasts, when I sought the right attitude so that I could change my job, this time, I simply wanted to have the right attitude to do my job. Wouldn't you know it: as the time to end my fast approached, I received a phone call from Paul Kroll, an editor for the *Plain Truth*. The Editorial Department was expanding, could I come in for an interview? I was hired to help Al Leiter, who managed the photo files, as a researcher.

I broke my fast with a cup of coffee, my first in more than two months. Chemistry professor Stig Erlander, who had been in Boston for the AAAS meetings, lectured on the evils of coffee in his nutrition class. I never took the class but received the lecture many times over from coeds in the dining hall serving line as I filled a cup from the urn. Finally, I decided to prove I was not addicted by going cold turkey. But now, with a job in Editorial, I knew of no better way to celebrate than with coffee.

That afternoon, shopping for a few items downtown, I spotted some Israeli coffee mugs, emblazoned with shields depicting the twelve tribes, two to a cup. I bought the one with the shield of Benjamin. In our Lost-Tribe mythology, that was the tribe that went to Scandinavia, home of my Viking ancestors. Just the thing to adorn my new desk. I shared an office with two others, Jack, layout artist for the publications, and Larry, an upper-class student who also did photo research.

And for my new job I had to begin wearing a tie. Nowadays, the occasions I put on a necktie are rare, but in those days, I noticed who walked around our campus in laid-back Southern California with a tie and who didn't. Now I was one of those who did.

But more than the tie, I felt I was where I belonged, working for a magazine. All the childhood hours spent leafing through old stacks of *Life* and *Look* stored in the cabinets underneath built-in bookshelves in the family room, then my major in photojournalism at B.U. all seemed to have prepared me for this.

I wasn't so blind that I would have called the *Plain Truth* the best magazine in the world, but it was, to me, the most important. With a circulation of three million and growing, it was certainly not insignificant. For the past two years, feeling that the broadcast and the magazine had come close to saturation of the audience that could be reached with religious language, there had been a conscious diminution of overtly religious content in the magazine, as well as on the telecast. This permitted World-wide to advertise in channels that didn't accept religious advertising, but it didn't please some of the top ministers, who saw this as watering down. A new magazine, *Tomorrow's World*, began and was offered to co-workers and others who desired more religious content.

The editorial mix may have changed, but the *Plain Truth* remained stodgy. Still, there were hopeful signs. Younger writers and researchers joined the staff. Twenty years earlier, Herbert Armstrong had produced the magazine himself. Although he suffered under the strain of doing this—in addition to the responsibility for his few congregations in the Pacific Northwest, the demands of his radio program, and the labor of getting Ambassador College off the ground—it had not been easy for him to let go and permit some of the new graduates of the college to have a hand in writing. Herman Hoeh made the first inroads, followed by others. Now there was a new wave of expansion.

A driving force in this was Paul Kroll. His title was associate editor, but he did the work that on other magazines would have carried the title managing editor. Paul was an extremely hard worker and could write with facility and flair. Another frequent contributor, Bill Dankenbring, wrote dull copy by comparison, but he could dependably turn out vast amounts of it on almost any topic; he was a writing machine. The names of still-newer writers were buried near the bottom of the masthead. Most of those at the top had two or three other responsibilities. There was no clear division between the church, the college, and the media outreach program; it was all the Work. Many of the evangelists had difficulty finding time to research and write the articles that ran under their names. In the lead-up to the transformation, some of the younger writers such as Gary Alexander began ghosting for the bigger names.

I threw myself into my work. Al had begun learning

computer programming and was in the process of tagging our files digitally for quick access. This meant he was happy for my help, assigning me to contact the Associated Press and other agencies for the photos we needed.

One of my first coups was a color photo of Winston Churchill during wartime. It was long thought that no color photos existed of him from that time. We ran it on the cover of *Tomorrow's World*.

As part of the effort to upgrade the magazine, the church booked Earl Theisen from *Look* for a series of seven weekly seminars, beginning at the end of January. This was the first time that writers, photographers, editors, and press personnel had met together for a training seminar. Each meeting was a four-hour block from ten to two, with a quick break for a bag lunch. It quickly became clear how helpful it would be to have input from a professional who viewed us from the outside yet felt that our magazine had a mission in an age of confusion to help people understand their world and themselves. At the same time, he challenged us to improve. One of the problems he diagnosed was a lack of communication and teamwork, masked by an excess of respect. At one point, after listening to people who had worked together for years address each other as "Mister", he cried out in exasperation, "Who do you people pray to? Mr. Christ?"

The *Portfolio* also had its own office space now in the Editorial Department (the year before, we had worked after-hours on the desks of others). Now we were in a windowless area in the northwest corner of the third floor of the Hall of Administration. Keith Stump, in his senior year, was the new editor (though called managing editor). I functioned as managing editor, with the title of associate editor, and we set to work with the array of new machines that enabled us to follow the lead of the Big Sandy *Portfolio* and produce camera-ready pages for the press. We used an IBM Selectric Composer. The Selectric was a top-of-the-line electric typewriter known for the interchangeable type on a head the size of a golf ball. The Composer was a version that used proportionately-spaced letters to produce justified columns. A typist entered our articles, then we ran the sheets of paper through a waxer that put ribbons of wax on the back. We then trimmed our columns of type and affixed them carefully to layout boards on a light table. A Varityper produced headlines. We also printed our photos to size but didn't affix them to the layout boards, as they were treated separately at the press. It was a lot of work to get each week's issue ready, but the results satisfied us.

We often worked late each week on the night before our next issue was due at the press. Once after working late, I laid down in my bed next to a window in my dorm, then woke in the half-light, amazed that I felt so refreshed at dawn. But I was mistaken; it was evening twilight. I had slept through the day and never noticed a thing.

With the transfer to Editorial, my second year at Ambassador began auspiciously. There was also no longer confusion as to whether I should identify with the freshmen or with the seniors (that bothersome designation "first-year senior" that we graduates of other colleges bore when we entered seemed to have fallen into disuse). I identified with the junior class, with whom I had most of my classes and would, barring mishap, graduate within a year and nine months. And we were able to get the administration to agree to allow five of us interested in the German language to live in one dorm. The approval came with reluctance; the administration believed in the benefits of having a cross-section in each dorm room. They had a point, but other colleges had foreign-language houses to facilitate study, so eventually, they agreed. We were in one of the townhouses that stood in a row perpendicular to the now-closed Grove Street.

One thing I enjoyed about the dorm was the possibility of opening windows in the bedroom. In the summer, I had been in the only residence hall kept open between school years, Grove Terrace. Unlike the other residences, it was newly-built as a dorm, which made it the most modern. That was nice in a way, but I had trouble getting used to the air conditioning. Some evenings I slept on the narrow balcony outside the study area.

Fall semester 1971 heralded the return of Herman Hoeh to a larger course load. He taught the third-year Bible course, as well as a course entitled The Ancient World. The backbone of that course was his so-called *Compendium*, a two-volume revision of ancient history based on old genealogies drawn up in the Middle Ages to trace the ancestries of the monarchs of that time to ancient heroes such as the kings of Troy. This class was taught early in the morning, in a free-association style. The benefit of taking both courses was that sometimes Hoeh started Third Year Bible in the middle of a train of thought he had begun to develop in the earlier class, to the mystification of students who only took the Bible course.

The third-year Bible course was called Theological Research. We learned the Hebrew and Greek alphabets and the use of basic reference works, preferably those that didn't suffer from the influence of "German higher criticism." It was axiomatic for Worldwide to maintain that the scriptures of the Old and New Testaments were error-free "in their original form." This made it crucial to know which was the right text. In the case of the Old Testament, this meant the Masoretic Hebrew text, which was not a controversial position.

For the New Testament, however, Hoeh asserted that the Greek Orthodox church had been divinely entrusted with the task of preserving the "correct" text, and had carried it out as faithfully as the rabbis had done with the Hebrew text. This position meant rejecting more than a century of developments in textual criticism as more ancient manuscripts came to light and revealed variants, some of which cast another light on beloved proof texts taken from the King James Bible.

Another lengthy unit in the course was the Hebrew calendar. This was important for Worldwide since, in addition to the weekly Sabbath, it also observed the annual festivals of the Old Testament. These observances are dated according to the lunar-solar calendar used by the Jews, rather than the commonly used Roman calendar. We were examined on our proficiency at correctly calculating the equivalent Roman calendar dates for any year past or future.

I signed up for Epistles of Paul, since Ron Dart, its teacher, had a high reputation among students for the depth of his exegesis (that's what they meant, but none of us used that term). The class was overbooked, though, so there was a call for ten students to switch to Old Testament Survey (OTS), which had free places. I reasoned that as a junior, I would have another chance to take Dart's course. This turned out to be wrong, however. By the time my senior year came, his duties supervising the ministry in international areas had left no time for teaching. OTS was an equally rewarding course in its own way, whenever David Jon Hill showed up. He had a gift for making the Old Testament narratives come to life in his humorous, even irreverent style. Given his other duties, however, he often sent his assistant, Orlin Grabbe, whom I had come to know from journalism class the year before.

There were two term papers for that course. In the fall semester, we had to write a paper on the modern identity of the ten lost tribes of Israel (fundamental to Worldwide's adherence to British Israelism and the idiosyncratic interpretation of prophecy resulting from that). In the spring semester, the assignment was "Job and I." Worldwide had its own take on the problem of the perplexing book of Job, in which a righteous man suffers torments he can't see any reason for. In addition to "solving" the question of the identity of this ancient patriarch (fourth-dynasty Pharaoh Khufu, Greek Cheops, buried in the Great Pyramid of Gizeh), the church claimed to know why Job suffered: self-righteousness. Herbert Armstrong had delineated this many years earlier in an article, "Why Must Men Suffer?" The title hints at the reason for the required OTS paper: Arrogance was not Job's sin alone, but the besetting sin of all mankind.

The time of writing this paper fell during one of the most trying times in my years in Pasadena, as will become clear. I poured out my heart while writing it, confessing the degree of my self-righteousness.

After these two papers were read and graded, they were placed in a stack at the foot of the student mail-slots in the Student Center, from which each of us could retrieve ours. That worked fine in the fall semester, so I know that my paper, "Where on Earth Did God Hide Those Tribes?"

received an excellent grade. I don't know my grade for "Job and I"—I couldn't find it in the stack. I have no idea who might have been interested enough in my life to carry off this paper.

Together with the rest of the male juniors, I took Advanced Public Speaking. The entire group met once a week at 8 A.M. for a lecture, then twice a week in small groups, where we delivered our speeches and received evaluations. I have three memories of that class. The first is about the weekly lecture. One week, the main lecturer couldn't make it; Clint Zimmermann, a former chiropractor and now a minister, substituted. It was another one of those mornings when I carried on a conversation at breakfast a little too long and had to rush up the hill to the Science hall. Having arrived too late, I tried to surreptitiously slip in a door at the rear of the lecture hall. I hadn't been the first late arrival, however, nor was I the last. Dr. Zimmerman reddened, chewed us out, and dismissed the class.

My next memory involves my "heart-to-heart" speech. I asked a classmate with whom I hadn't had much to do what he wanted to know about me. He answered: "Why do you smile so much?" It was a helpful question. Reflecting on it, I realized for the first time how important it had been to my father to have a son. He saw combat in the Pacific, and holding his child was evidence for him that the war was really over. Apparently, I had a sunny disposition from birth. But by the time I was in grade school, I didn't always feel like smiling. I can remember trooping down the stairs, not quite awake, grumpy that I had to go to school. My dad ordered me to march back upstairs and come back with a smile on my face.

The third memory is an evaluation of one of my speeches from Howard Clark. He told me I wandered around my topic like a wounded buffalo. Instead, giving a speech should be like shooting an arrow. The feathers on the arrow are not tangents, but serve to keep the arrow on course. The same applies to any details we bring into a speech.

In the fall semester, I also took a new one-semester course, Management. As the Work grew in complexity, the entrepreneurial style Herbert Armstrong used in the early days, when he knew all ministers and employees personally, was no longer effective. Some saw the solution in the growing body of literature in the new field of management. So along with the Bible, that semester, I read Peter Drucker, Doug MacGregor, and others. I was fascinated by the view of human nature in their writings. MacGregor contrasted two underlying sets of assumptions about people. In the first of these, theory x, people are by nature lazy and have to be closely supervised. In the second, theory y, people thrive on achievement and can be motivated. The second view appealed to me, despite its implicit rejection of the deceitful heart, desperately wicked (Jer. 17:9) view of human nature often preached from the pulpit.

In the spring semester, I took another one-semester course, Family Relations. David Antion was the nominal teacher, but often his assistant Les Stocker substituted. So, for two of my courses that year, there was the nominal teacher of the course listings and the substitute who showed up most days. On top of this, there was a turnover between semesters. Richard Plache, still under a cloud after the love-in a few months earlier, was relieved as Dean of Students and then, in the middle of the spring semester, sent to England. In return, Ernest Martin came to Pasadena from England. Martin was a friendly, red-faced southerner, and the best-organized teacher I had in Pasadena. He completed the second semester of third-year Bible, Herman Hoeh having returned to his other duties. Many professors waded through the semester's script, left off when time ran out, and picked up again the next time the class met. Martin, however, planned his course as discrete units. For each class, he knew exactly what he wanted to get across during the hour, and when he was done, so did we.

In the course of that school year, my sixth year in college, and my eighteenth overall, I finally learned how to turn in papers on time. Until then, when I sat down to write the evening before an assignment was due, I was at a loss for ideas. I usually ground something out, and more than once, I missed a deadline or even had to take an incomplete. I noticed that I had more ideas for these papers than I realized. They would strike me at odd times, though—in the shower, walking to class, standing in line at the dining hall, even during a different class. My new strategy involved taking a fresh manila folder the day a paper was assigned, labeling it, and placing in it all the details of the assignment, then placing the folder in my desk drawer. Then, as thoughts came to me over the next weeks, I wrote them on slips of paper (even paper napkins for the ideas that came during a meal) and threw them into the folder. Then, when I started to write (often still on the evening before the due date), I would be amazed at the amount and quality of ideas. This may sound pathetically banal, but it changed my life. I wish I had learned to do this ten years earlier.

Chapter Eight

As auspicious as fall 1971 was for me personally, there was an underlying tension on campus about what January 1972 would bring. The world as we knew it might tumble down around us. Or not.

Many Christians are convinced that Jesus will return "soon." Worldwide was one of those groups that thought it could put a number on his return. Based on interpretation of data in the prophetic and apocalyptic books of the Bible, and using assumptions such as "a day for a year" and the obscure references to 1260, 1290, and 1335 days at the end of the Book of Daniel (Dan. 12:7–13; the "time, times and a half" of verse 7 correspond to the 1260 days) common among prophecy buffs, the church was convinced Jesus would return on the Feast of Trumpets in 1975.

Immediately preceding this would be a "half-week" (Dan. 9:27), interpreted as three-and-a-half years, of tribulation. Again, in our KJV-inspired jargon, the Great Tribulation. That would begin in spring 1972.

Other groups, notably, the Watchtower Society (Jehovah's Witnesses), looked to the same date, but for Worldwide, it was corroborated by considerations specific to its own history and the Metonic cycle. Meton, an Athenian astronomer and contemporary of Socrates, was apparently the first to calculate that nineteen years is the shortest sequence of time that can bring solar and lunar years in alignment so that the moon phases recur on the same days of the solar year. So, periods of nineteen years must be significant as well, and Worldwide believed it was no coincidence that Herbert Armstrong's broadcasting career began—after filling a few open slots for a morning devotional on a Eugene radio station in fall 1933—on the first Sunday in January 1934. Nineteen years later, on the first Sunday in January 1953, Armstrong's program, which had first been called the *Radio Church of God* (lending its name to the church that grew out of it), but now called the *World Tomorrow*, first aired in Europe on Radio Luxembourg. Nineteen years after that, January 7, 1972, was coming fast and would fall 1335 days before Trumpets 1975.

Worldwide saw a parallel to this in the history of the first-century church. According to its reconstruction of New Testament chronology, the church began its public preaching on Pentecost in the year 31 (recorded in Acts 2). The mission to Europe, which began with Paul's trip to Philippi, recorded in Acts 16, was dated in this reconstruction to Pentecost of the year 50, nineteen years later. Nineteen years after that, according to a tradition recorded by two fourth-century church historians, the Jerusalem Christians fled across the Jordan River to Pella, shortly before the Roman destruction of the city, ending the first, golden era of the church after two nineteen-year cycles.

Similarly, Worldwide expected to flee to a place of safety in January 1972. This is something I knew nothing about until after I began attending services. Some may have learned about this beforehand and became baptized to become part of the chosen few who would be spared in the Tribulation. When I was baptized, though, it was with the conviction that I had sealed my fate to be one of those hunted and persecuted when the German-led final revival of the Holy Roman Empire invaded America. But now, I learned otherwise. God would supernaturally remove the faithful from danger, not through a heavenly rapture, but hidden in a safe place on earth, Petra, in the south Jordanian desert, the ancient capital of the Hasmonean kingdom.

For years, the timetable that the Great Tribulation would begin in 1972 seemed plausible. In the 1960s, it had been easy to believe that the world could not long continue as it was. In addition to the threat of mutual annihilation from the opponents in the Cold War, now the U.S. was involved in a war in Vietnam, one that it was not winning. In reaction to the war, college campuses were in turmoil, coming on the heels of the upheaval from riots in the ghettos of many cities. John F. Kennedy's assassination was followed by the deaths of his brother Bobby, Martin Luther King, Jr., and others. On top of this, it was the Swinging Sixties, with increasingly open experimentation in sex and drugs. In an event that seemed to have unmistakable significance as a fulfillment of prophecy, not only for Worldwide but for the wider community of dispensationalist fundamentalists, was Israel's astounding victory in the Six-Day War, clearing the way for the construction of the third temple, to which the messiah would return. An eager tourist tried to help history along by fire-bombing the Al Aksa mosque on the Temple Mount. It soon turned out that he was a Worldwide co-worker who had unsuccessfully sought baptism. News photos showing him with recent issues of the *Plain Truth* in his cell were an embarrassment for the church.

On the other hand, some pieces of the jigsaw puzzle did not seem to fit. In particular, the European Community seemed to lag. Worldwide was not alone in seeing this as the latest incarnation of the Holy Roman Empire. Hadn't the organization been founded by the Treaty of Rome? Yet expansion had stalled, Britain (in Worldwide's understanding, one of the main "Israelite" nations), was poised to join. Yet the organization was still short of the ten nations it would need to have (based on the ten horns of the Beast of Rev. 13:1). Above all, a common foreign and defense policy was lagging. NATO didn't include all EC nations and was led by the United States. Even though Germany had demonstrated its mastery of the sudden attack in both world wars, contributing the word *Blitzkrieg* to the English language, it seemed increasingly unlikely that it could successfully launch an invasion of North America in spring 1972.

Herbert Armstrong quietly ratcheted down Worldwide's expectations. He still felt the dates were possible but viewed them as less and less likely. He had Rod Meredith, superintendent of ministry, instruct pastors to cautiously pass the message to their congregations; the flight to safety would probably not happen in 1972, though the end remained imminent.

Ted Armstrong, in his Feast sermon in 1970, speculated that we may have been wrong on many details of our end-time scenario. Yet surprisingly, rather than saying it might be further in the future than we had thought, he concluded: "It's coming to the point when I no longer can preach with conviction Christ can't come tonight" (this a reference to Billy Graham's emotional appeal at the conclusion of his crusades, that Christ might come tonight). On top of that, when we went through Daniel and Revelation in second-year Bible, it turned out there was some wiggle-room. Did the seven years of Nebuchadnezzar's madness (Dan. 4:28–37) count or not?

Still, there was no official word that we were not fleeing, so many of us thought it still might happen that we would attend the fall semester in Pasadena, then spring semester in the Jordanian desert, the place of final training Gerald Waterhouse talked about. We cautiously admitted to each other that, when packing for the Feast of Tabernacles that fall, we had considered what we would have in our suitcases if the days were cut short (Matt. 24:22) and the order to flee came while we were assembled at the feast sites. The logistics of our going from these few locations around the world would be simpler than if we all had to leave from our homes. It was as if we lived in two dimensions of reality. On the world scene, there was no indication of an imminent crisis. Yet Jesus had warned the end coming at a time we would least expect it (Matt. 24:44) so that lack of crisis was no disconfirmation. We simply had to wait and see. At least I didn't suffer from the nightmare some of my classmates reported: they had dreamed that the flight had taken place and they had been left behind.

Adding to the tension was a sense of struggle between the two Armstrongs. Herbert Armstrong scolded us for behavioral lapses, while Ted Amstrong seemed impatient with the micromanagement of the lives of students and members. Once Keith and I half-seriously considered headlining a *Portfolio* report of two successive student forums, "Chancellor Says Get Back, Vice-Chancellor Says Not So Far."

New Year's Day 1972 fell on a Sabbath. The chorale sang for church services in El Monte, where Leroy Neff's sermon balanced between a reasonable tone and maintaining a commitment to prophecy, if not to a specific timetable. He began by advising us to always expect the unexpected. "Don't decide how things are going to develop. You know the conclusion of many things, but you don't know how it's going to get that way." This was both sensible and disingenuous. The timetables were not the work of lay members, but of Herbert Armstrong and his top lieutenants. If we had a scenario in mind, it was one painted for us in church literature and sermons. He ended by alluding to the parable of wise and foolish virgins in the gospel (Matt. 25:1–13), admonishing us, "Be prepared: now is the time to get your oil ready—to watch, pray, study, do the work. Set your spiritual house in order."

Meanwhile, Ted Armstrong had given the afternoon sermon in the Pasadena gym that doubled as college chapel. I listened to the tape recording a couple of days later. His opening: We cannot base our conduct on chronology. Instead, we need to be more Christ-centered.

Nevertheless, we couldn't help but assemble in a state of agitation and expectation for Bible study Friday evening, January 7, 1972, the date that concluded the second of the church's two nineteen-year time cycles. It was conducted by the troika of Herbert Armstrong, Stan Rader, and Ted Armstrong. And yes, Herbert Armstrong announced he had big news for us: our ads would now be accepted in the U.S. by *Reader's Digest*, which had previously not accepted religious advertising. The overseas editions didn't have that restriction, and ads in *Reader's Digest* had been one of the church's most productive sources of new subscribers. The toning down of overtly religious articles in the *Plain Truth* had achieved what he had hoped.

It was an important opening, but we could be pardoned if we felt a bit let-down. Even more strangely, the second major announcement was that the final loan to guarantee construction for a college auditorium had come through. One week later, January 14, we attended the groundbreaking for it, meant to be the crowning jewel of the campus, a campus we had thought we would be abandoning that week. Yet here was Herbert Armstrong with a silver construction helmet and a silver shovel, beaming his round-faced smile for cameras as we stood and watched. The justification, for those who wondered, was the saying of Jesus, recorded in Matt. 24:46: "Blessed the servant whom his master finds so doing." This was similar to the quotation attributed to Martin Luther after World War II: "If I knew the world were to end tomorrow, I would plant an acorn today" (many people have said many memorable things, but over time, through some kind of magnetic attraction, they become attributed to Abraham Lincoln, Winston Churchill, or Martin Luther—or Yogi Berra). Of course, Herbert Armstrong was doing more than planting an acorn when he pushed the shovel into the ground and turned over the first spade of earth.

The auditorium was one of two projects that had long been on the drawing boards, as demonstrated by a model of the master plan for the campus displayed in the lobby of the Hall of Administration. The other was a proper college library. The original college building—the old Fowler-McCormick mansion—couldn't house the library the college would need if it sought accreditation. Whereas for the auditorium, no expense was spared (at $12 million, that worked out to more than $10,000 per seat), there never seemed to be enough money for the library. The college did begin some additional, smaller projects, such as tearing out the tennis courts between the student center and the gym to replace them with a parking facility covered with a track that featured the first installation of artificial turf in Southern California.

At about the same time, construction on the long-delayed Long Beach freeway, I-210, began. The church's press and other buildings that stood in its way had to be torn down. The new press building, as well as the church's private K–12 school, Imperial, and a new office building, were cut off from the main campus. To get there, we used a pedestrian overpass over the freeway construction. The church also opened a commissary and a new insurance agency. These reinforced the impression that we weren't going anywhere soon.

Within weeks, there was a more surprising turn of events, but not a positive one. Ted Armstrong's sermon at the Feast of Tabernacles in the fall of 1971 had been perhaps the best I ever heard from him, emotional without being histrionic. He began by playing the Jackie DeShannon hit from a few years previously, "What the World Needs Now Is Love."

The notion may have been a commonplace outside of Worldwide, with its focus on commandment-keeping. Ted Armstrong, at the top of his speaking form, criticized the church's habit of stressing obedience to the rules instead of practicing love, not only within the church but as active concern for the well-being of those outside the church. He concluded with an appeal: "What the world needs now is us." Given the reaction my then-fiancée and I had to the first Worldwide service we attended four years earlier, I was receptive to it. Yet it was ironic given Ted Armstrong's reaction when Richard Plache had arrived at a similar diagnosis months earlier.

Then we heard Herbert Armstrong had forbidden his son to speak the next day in Penticton, B.C., or for the rest of his planned Feast schedule. The word was that he was under strain (the term Plache had used at the time of the love-in). He went on an unannounced leave of absence, returned to Pasadena in December, but in February was placed on leave again, this time announced to the public. We were told that he needed a rest. I hadn't given it much thought in December when the new office of deputy chancellor was created for the Pasadena campus. Each of the other two campuses had a deputy chancellor (Herbert Armstrong was chancellor of all three). We hadn't been told that Ted Armstrong was no longer vice-chancellor. But if he was overworked, some delegation of college administration seemed sensible. David Antion, who had been Ted Armstrong's administrative assistant (as well as being his brother-in-law) and supervisor of the Press, filled the new office.

Ted Armstrong's sudden disappearance from the airwaves in February earned the church unwelcome media attention. Russell Chandler, religion writer for the *Los Angeles Times*, wrote more than one article, and *Time* covered it in its May 15 edition, entitled "Garner Ted, Where Are You?" (a play on the title of the popular sitcom of the time about two hapless policemen in *Car 54*). The article contained an accurate report of the church's teachings. Alongside mention of the observance of such Old Testament customs as Sabbath, the Passover, and keeping kosher, the article touched on the church's rejection of common Christian holidays and the doctrine of the Trinity. Reporter Sandra Burton fairly characterized the church as heterodox, rigid, and disciplined. We would have preferred that members of the general public not find out about things like three tithes, British-Israelism, end-time scenarios, and failed predictions until they had been prepared by reading literature that put these matters in what we felt was proper perspective. I smarted at the description of Ambassador College, "where the buildings are expensive and the tuition cheap."

In addition to background about Worldwide, the article implied that Ted Armstrong was banished because of unspecified moral lapses, which was reinforced by a second article that shared the religion page in that week's edition, entitled "Paul Tillich, Lover" (which was a misleading headline, since the article was more about the lifestyle and allegations of Mrs. Tillich).

I believe it was significant that both Ted Armstrong's misbehavior and the reaction to it came to a head in the immediate wake of the disconfirmation of the church's timeline for the end of the age. In other words, the way Ted Armstrong's call to preach Christ rather than chronology might have had as much to do with his banishment as the way he spent the night after giving the sermon (word eventually leaked that he had spent it in a Tahoe chalet with the flight attendant of his plane).

Meanwhile, the struggle to make sense of Worldwide's identity in the light of our non-flight made itself felt in another way. A logjam of doctrinal questions had built up. As long as the end might be imminent, one could put them aside, knowing that soon we could ask the returned Christ directly. Now, patience ebbed.

One controversial topic was the correct date for keeping Pentecost, which Ernest Martin had long contended we were keeping on the wrong day (Monday) when it should be kept on Sunday. Herbert Armstrong, defending the church's interpretation, maintained that to keep it on the wrong day was as bad as not keeping it at all. Noting that in the account of the day of Pentecost in the Book of Acts, those who gathered in the crowd that day received the Holy Spirit, he suggested that those not congregating with the church on the "right" day now didn't have access to the divine gift. This categorical assertion made it difficult to approach the question dispassionately.

Other questions came from field ministers and centered on issues that impacted the lives of congregants and prospective members. One was the reliance on divine healing. When would it be a sin or lack of faith to seek help from the medical profession? Another was the strict stance on divorce and remarriage. Worldwide's understanding of the relevant scriptures was similar to that of the Roman Catholic Church. The impact, however, was greater. For one thing, there are many more Catholics than members of Worldwide, making for a larger pool of potential mates. For another, most who are Catholic are so from birth and know before entering marriage what the teaching is. In Worldwide's case, many came into contract with its teaching after marrying and divorcing, then remarrying according to civil law. More than one couple separated from a spouse to come into the church because of a previous marriage; many others found the hurdle too high and turned away sorrowfully. A third issue was the hardship many experienced because of Worldwide's insistence on three tithes, all taken from the gross. As the number of members outside the U.S. grew, many living in nations with much higher tax rates, the problem became more acute. There were questions about the biblical basis for all three teachings. Some ministers might have had no problem administering these teachings if they could be certain that the teachings were sound, while others reasoned either that God wouldn't have let Herbert Armstrong be wrong about these things, or that, if he were, then God would show him.

Herbert Armstrong, rather than addressing any of this, spoke instead about a fourth issue troubling some. A group promoting sacred names, the idea that God would only listen to someone addressing him with a Hebrew name, had made inroads in some congregations. This is something Armstrong had combatted in his early years, so he could fall back on his previous research.

Meanwhile, the broadcasts continued, but with reruns of older radio programs Herbert Armstrong had done. The church had about a year's worth in its archives, made in the years before Ted Armstrong became the voice of the *World Tomorrow*. We were told that Herbert Armstrong would begin recording new programs as well. Members enjoyed hearing the older programs again. They were well-structured sermons, which some felt were an improvement over Ted Armstrong's free-association style. But mail response dropped. These rerun programs did not pull in new listeners and readers at the same rate as Ted Armstrong's.

Equally worrying, the church's income dipped. Announcements about this during services included speculation about several possible reasons, without ever mentioning three: uncertainty in the minds of some over what had happened to Ted Armstrong, questions about why members needed to sacrifice to build a concert hall, and the effect of the postponement of the end of the world. Members had gone above and beyond their means in the belief that time was short. But if we were going to be here a few more years, then teeth needed fixing, and children needed new shoes.

The practice of not mentioning the obvious extended to us on the *Portfolio* staff. I don't recall any discussion about how to report the sudden disappearance of the vice-chancellor of the college, the public face of the church's outreach efforts. When the head of the Romanian writer's union visited the campus and spoke at an assembly earlier that year, Keith and I speculated it would have been interesting to have a symposium with him on the role of the press in a controlled society. But in the case of Ted Armstrong's leave of absence, we had so internalized the expectations and limits on us that it was obvious we wouldn't be reporting it. The closest we came to acknowledging it was the photo we ran to accompany a report on Herbert Armstrong's return from his latest world trip. Don Lorton,

144

one of the many fine photographers who worked for the *Plain Truth*, had recorded the scene as the G-II touched down in Glendale. Members of the executive committee met the plane. The photo showed Herbert Armstrong and Stan Rader, both having just disembarked, in conversation with them, heads bowed, brows furrowed. It didn't require a fertile imagination to know what they were discussing.

Nevertheless, we carried on. After all, we were doing the "Work."

One week in late February, I learned that we had gotten a fact wrong in a front-page story of the *Portfolio*. The galleys had been delivered to Pre-press that morning. I called the department manager, explained the situation, and asked him if it would be possible to bring over a revised headline and opening paragraph. He said that they had not yet begun work on it and that if I could be there within an hour, it would not throw them off schedule.

I was happy that we could run an accurate article and thankful for the uncomplicated flexibility of the Pre-press Department. But not everyone was happy. We had a new faculty advisor that year. He was on the staff of the *Plain Truth*, specializing in science articles. He also taught the journalism class. I was in no position to judge his science qualifications, but I had a negative view of his journalism skills; perhaps I didn't hide it well. At any rate, tension grew. Every week, there was some disagreement between us when he reviewed the galleys before they went to press.

Now I was called into Paul Kroll's office and told that I was fired from the Editorial Department. The faculty advisor had stormed into Paul's office, claiming that I had shown up at the press, shouting, "stop the presses." He issued an ultimatum: "Either Henry goes, or I do." Given a choice between a full-time employee and a student, Paul's decision made sense. I was dismissed as one of the editors of the paper as well. It also meant that I couldn't attend the rest of the Theisen seminars, which disappointed me.

It was humiliating to be the only student on campus without a job. Rather than blaming the faculty advisor, I looked for the fault in myself and set about trying to learn whatever it was that God wanted to show me. Reading the Bible as much as we did, it was natural that there were some characters we felt more connected with than others. In my case, there were two: Joseph and Peter. Joseph, one of the twelve sons of Jacob, was a dreamer, and naively recounted dreams that suggested that his life held big things in store. In his simplicity, he seemed unaware of how those hearing him—especially his brothers—would react. He had much growing up to do. As for Peter, the connection I felt was not that he was the leading apostle, but that he was irrepressible. He was the first to speak up, which more than once landed him in difficulty.

The timing of my dismissal seemed appropriate, as well. We were in the weeks before our annual observance of the Lord's Supper on the Passover, and each year we were admonished to examine ourselves in preparation for it. There was no doubt in my mind that God was chastening me, humbling me, and I found ample reason why he might do so.

Still, it was a bitter experience. I had loved my job and felt I was making a contribution to the Work. I walked much more softly around the campus, which was fitting, given the generally somber atmosphere.

The role of the Personnel Department had changed. I was on my own in looking for a job and had to apply independently to various departments, where I was told budgets were frozen because of the drop in donations. No one verbalized it, but perhaps one or two department heads thought if I had been fired, I must be more trouble than I was worth, and they didn't want to take over someone else's problem.

Finally, I received a tip from Dan Porter, whose management class I had taken that year. He had dreams of upgrading the student center into a service center. That would involve revamping the bookstore, which could easily use its space to carry three times as many titles as it did. Until then, it had limited its offerings to "safe" titles such as nineteenth-century Bible reference works. Someone with my work experience, both the several years in my dad's delicatessen and the summer spent in a bookstore near Harvard Square, seemed like a good profile to realize his vision. He wanted me to learn the operation of the student center from the bottom up and advised me to apply to Food Services. I called the manager, Bill Mott, and was also interviewed by Bill Schuetz, who supervised the student workers, a crusty, golden-hearted man. They decided they could use another male student in the crew. Most of the food service workers were girls, but for carrying heavy things in and out of the freezer, they liked to have at least one guy on call during all shifts. An additional duty they preferred to assign to a man: feeding Hobart, the large dishwashing machine hidden in a back corner. The Hobart company also manufactured the scales we used in the delicatessen, so I felt at home. After each meal, at least one male worked scullery, taking the trays as students deposited them on a conveyer belt, scraping the plates, tossing paper goods, separating items, and placing them in the gaping maw of Hobart.

The work was as physically demanding as custodial had been, perhaps slightly more so, but it was job-content I knew something about. Sometimes when the crew was short a person, I filled in on the serving line, helping "feed the flock," lightheartedly misapplying the admonition in 1 Pet. 5:2. Occasionally, I filled in serving in faculty dining, normally done by finely-groomed coeds. At least once, I was asked to open the champagne bottles at an evening function hosted by Mr. Armstrong. The names on the label, Moët & Chandon, brought back memories of my visit to their caves in France in the summer of 1964.

148

Most of all, I was happy to no longer be the only unemployed student on campus. The same week I got that job, there was another unexpected turn. Herbert Armstrong asked Kevin Dean to cut his senior year short to serve as the steward on the G-II. Kevin was treasurer in my Ambassador Club, and I was appointed in his place. Normally, all the club officers were seniors. The only exception that year was my friend Randy, a club president. Now I was the second junior with a club office. This all made sense in the frame of reference we all used to interpret what we experienced: God had humbled me by putting me through a severe trial, and now restored me. It was a pattern familiar to us from the Book of Job.

My friend Randy, also junior class president, also went through some soul-searching at the time, along with many others in our class. Each year, the grad ball was the responsibility of the junior class. When it was our turn, we wanted to top everything previously done. It seemed, however, that there were obstacles everywhere. Topping the list: New Year's Day had fallen on a Sabbath that year, so revenue that usually came through parking, concessions, program sales and other activities during the Rose Bowl Parade was lost. The student body fund was low. Randy took a step back, threw out everything planned so far, and reassembled the planning group. Our internal motto would now be "wash feet." Since we were all conversant with the action of Jesus in the Gospel of John on his last evening with his disciples, were understood: We were to adopt an attitude of service rather than seeking to impress everyone. And the resulting ball turned out fine—an important lesson for us.

One more thing made the spring semester of my junior year special. I grew ever-closer to another of the "first-year seniors" who entered the same time as I. We had found from the first, during a hike in Yosemite on the way to the Feast of Tabernacles 1970, that we had much in common. Margie had been an English Lit major at her previous college. She could talk of her love for Shakespeare without sounding pretentious. In keeping with the rules, we took care not to spend too much time together and dated widely.

Margie taught English at Imperial High School, the private school operated by the church for the children of its employees. It turned out she was a gifted teacher, and highly regarded by the students. Combined with her previous college, she had enough credits to graduate, so she was reclassified as a senior, which would enable her to take a full teaching load the next year. Since she was in her last semester, this meant it was all right for her to get serious. We saw each other often, and I began to look into what it would mean to be a married student for my senior year. We were discrete about it, but we saw each other regularly.

An additional benefit for her was to have a person she could trust with her confidences. Her best friend was the coed and flight attendant involved with Ted Armstrong before his banishment. Herbert Armstrong knew this and called Margie into his office and put the fear of God into her to not spread gossip, but she knew she could trust me not to repeat what she told me.

Others have since documented allegations that Ted Armstrong had bedded other coeds before our classmate, but we didn't know that at the time because Herbert Armstrong had successfully silenced previous cases. He accused the women, asking what they had done to provoke his son. The interrogation and intimidation Margie endured simply by being the friend and confidante of his son's current flame made it easy for me to imagine what Ted Armstrong's previous conquests endured from Armstrong senior. At the time, I assumed that I was one of the few who knew; no one else found out about it from me. This knowledge meant I should pray fervently for our classmate, and also for Ted and Shirley Armstrong.

King David in the Bible had stumbled badly in a similar way, I reminded myself. Looking back, it's strange to realize how we revered the Armstrongs and that we put Ted Armstrong on the level of the greatest king of Israel. Why that would allow him to exercise *droit du seigneur* on the coeds was something I didn't ask myself. And at the time, I only knew of one coed, so I thought it was a one-time lapse, which could happen to anyone. At B.U., faculty coed romances happened. It was a common sight to see one prominent professor zooming through Kenmore Square in his convertible sports car with a lovely coed in the passenger seat. But Ted Armstrong was not just a college administrator, he was a married minister who both in sermons and on the airwaves flailed away against the very behavior he was engaging in.

Now, after learning of earlier escapades, I wonder what was different in 1972 that led Herbert Armstrong to banish his son. Perhaps, in this case, gossip was spreading too widely for Herbert Armstrong to suppress it. It wasn't long before a British tabloid publicized the "love storm" around the handsome televangelist. Besides, this was apparently the first time Ted Armstrong expressed his intention to divorce his wife, in defiance of the church's strict teaching.

It's easy to understand that some with knowledge of Ted Armstrong's behavior were simply disgusted and could no longer refrain from complaining about it. There were grounds to seriously ask whether he was fit to be a minister, and this was asked in the upper echelons.

But there may have been an additional factor at play. In the Sixties, Worldwide focused on finishing its commission, racing against a rapidly approaching deadline. Now that deadline was inoperative. Where should the church go from here? The battle over its future direction played out in the positioning of its publications and the aims of its colleges.

Layered over philosophical differences were power

struggles. Herbert Armstrong was a few months from turning 80. Ted Armstrong was the heir apparent and was wary of the most ambitious who vied for his father's ear, men such as Rod Meredith and Stan Rader. Was Ted Armstrong the object of strategic leaks?

Chapter Nine

Ted Armstrong's banishment was a crucial moment in the history of the church. All of us who were committed to Worldwide as "God's true church" were shaken. Coming so soon after the disconfirmation of the church's reckoning for the time of the end, the revelation that the public face of Worldwide was a deeply flawed human was traumatic. Some were scandalized and left the church. Among those who remained, some adopted a more critical stance. I was among them at times, but more often continued to see Ted Armstrong as a latter-day King David, a man who had sinned grievously but sought to serve God. I believed what Paul wrote to the Romans: "For whatever things were written aforetime were written for our learning" (Rom. 15:4). The Bible was not only our primary academic text; it was relevant to our existence. In a palpable sense, we were living in Bible times. I took the Bible warnings seriously against judging and casting the first stone. I continued to see my own flaws—my brashness, my desire for attention, my lack of focus—leaving me little time to condemn Ted Armstrong. And I continued to believe that this was the work of God with a divine commission to warn the world of impending, though slightly delayed, doom. I wanted to have a part in that work.

What was the Work? Herbert Armstrong was faced with the choice of either confirming that it was the work of God, in which case no human was indispensable, or that it was the Armstrong family business. Pressuring him in his choice: income sank and responses to the radio broadcast, which now consisted of reruns of his old programs in place of Ted's, were down.

In retrospect, it's not surprising that Herbert Armstrong decided, with unseemly haste, that his son had repented sufficiently not only to be readmitted to the Church (there had never been official confirmation that he had been put out), but restored to all duties. At the time, I took it as an answer to prayer. The news came just after the school year ended. I was home in New Jersey for a short visit and heard it from an elder in the congregation there.

From the flurry of initiatives, policy decisions, and shuffling of personnel, it seemed as if Ted Armstrong had dictated the terms of his return. Not only would he resume daily radio programs but he also planned to place the telecast, until then weekly, daily in some markets. A new series of evangelistic campaigns termed "personal appearances" would begin in Calgary, Alba., in August. The format included a chorale and band drafted from both Pasadena and Big Sandy campuses. I was chosen as an alternate, so I learned the music but was never needed. It did get me an invitation to a cookout for the group shortly before the first campaign at Ted and Shirley Armstrong's home on Waverly Drive, not far from campus. This was my first experience of Ted and his wife in a private setting. Watching them share final preparations in the kitchen, I saw no hint of strain in their relationship, unless that was the reason for his attentiveness.

In addition to resuming his grueling broadcast schedule, Ted Armstrong quickly took executive control of every aspect of the Work. He sought to promote more open communication and a more collegial atmosphere in the administration—he called it a "shirt-sleeves" approach. He also pushed back against the secretive atmosphere of the church (local congregations met, for instance, in unmarked halls; their services were not listed in local papers). He got his father's approval to instruct local pastors that people were free to attend our services even if their interest was only casual. These were all policies he had long promoted; hardliners had stifled them before and remained skeptical. He initiated a project to organize the church's teaching on a systematic basis. This, too, was something that already had been under discussion. The church had published so much literature that there was confusion about just what it taught on some issues. For a church that marketed itself as having the right teaching (the "plain truth"), this was embarrassing.

There was an executive shuffle as well. Rod Meredith was removed from his job directing Church Administration, in which function he had been the main interface between the field ministry and headquarters during the crisis caused by Ted Armstrong's banishment. He traded jobs with Ted Armstrong's brother-in-law, David Antion, to become deputy chancellor of the college. One of Meredith's deputies, Dennis Luker, went to Australia to replace Wayne Cole, who took over another of the three jobs David Antion had held, that of press manager. No comparable assignment was found for the other of Meredith's two deputies, Al Carrozzo.

From what we students could see, Ted Armstrong settled into a working relationship with his father marked by a tense dynamic. Each recognized he needed the other, but the elder Armstrong remained suspicious of his son's lifestyle, and the son felt that his father was at the mercy of conflicting forces that sought to influence him, in part to block some reforms the younger Armstrong wished to introduce. Ted Armstrong felt that these influencers pushed his father into a stricter direction than was necessary. In this, they were reinforcing a trend in the elder Armstrong's personality. As Herbert Armstrong grew older and more remote, there was a struggle for access to him.

Ted Armstrong was a volatile factor. The plummet in response to the broadcast during his exile had proven—to him most of all—that he was indispensable to Worldwide. Now he wanted a free hand but chafed at his father's inconsistency. Herbert Armstrong often withdrew approval for a decision Ted Armstrong had run by him, claiming to have never heard of it. Ted Armstrong was frustrated by the moves of those who sought to interpose themselves between the two of them. His character flaws gave them ample grounds for trying to cut him off from effective executive power and to restrict his role to being the public face of the church. There was no doubt of his ability to attract new listeners and subscribers and bring in more co-workers and members. Whether he could be an effective administrator remained to be seen.

We students weren't privy to these inner struggles at the time, beyond the experience of announcements made one week and countermanded the next. The feeling of whiplash students and employees felt the year before continued.

It's hard to know if this upheaval would have taken place without Ted Armstrong's banishment and reinstatement. I believe it's likely it would have. With the disconfirmation of our prophetic timeline in January 1972, a struggle over the future of the church was inevitable. Some yearned for the good old days when a handful of ministers, all personally known to Herbert Armstrong, and a few thousand members were the church. Others understood that the combination of larger congregations and the prospect of more time in this world before Christ's return (still "imminent," of course), necessarily brought changes.

A recurring theme that summed up Ted Armstrong's theological approach was his perceived need for the church to be more Christ-centered. He didn't question Worldwide's allegiance to the Sabbath or other Old Testament strictures. But his understanding of the Sabbath controversies in the Gospels, for instance, indicated to him that they depict Jesus as one who advocated a more humane application of the command, not only in comparison to the way the religious leaders of his time practiced it but also to the way it was often taught in Worldwide.

My reaction to this turmoil wavered between gullible acceptance of the public explanations for these moves and growing cynicism, followed by renewed self-accusatory fasts for my know-it-all attitude.

These developments played out over the summer, which I spent again on campus after my visit home. A group of students traveled to Bad Oeynhausen for the second year of the German program, larger than the first year, and the largest group yet went to the Temple Mount dig. Again, I was not part of either. Nor was I among the small group of juniors who were sent for the summer to work as ministerial trainees, although a rumor reached Pasadena from Big Sandy that someone had seen my name on the list that circulated there. I never asked anyone why I had been stricken, While I could think of reasons why I might be on the list, I could think of even more for my removal. But none of that bothered me. Unlike a year earlier, when I had to struggle with my attitude while working as a custodian, I returned to my job in the kitchen and enjoyed it.

There were two of us male students working full-time in food services for the summer. This made larger jobs possible, such as emptying and cleaning the freezers. Our schedule called for us to alternate early and late shifts week by week, with an overlap in the middle of the day, when we did these larger jobs. The early shift began at six, the late shift ended when the Hobart was emptied after the evening meal. I did not adjust well to changing my rhythm each week. After a couple of weeks, it turned out that the other fellow had trouble getting in on time when he was on the early shift. One day I arrived when my shift started and found that day's milk delivery from Altadena Dairy still on the dock, in the sunshine. Since we used raw milk, this was not good. Rather than report my co-worker, I asked him if he would agree to change our work schedule. I was willing to come in early all summer. He, being a night person, didn't have to think long to agree. After that, I settled into a routine that worked for me.

This meant that I went to bed early. Margie had graduated and was now at the summer camp in Orr. Officially, we were no longer a pair—I had gotten cold feet. But she wanted to remain my friend rather than have no relationship with me, and I was happy to comply. Despite Ted Armstrong's restoration, the sense of crisis in the church continued. Margie could use an office telephone late at night, so many a time I got a call from her after I had gone to bed. I sat on the floor of the hall in Grove Terrace in my pajamas and talked with her, sometimes for hours. I didn't mind. My reluctance to commit hadn't changed how much she meant to me.

My contentment with my job in the kitchen made the shock even greater when, once again, I received a phone call from John Kilburn. The Photography Department was being reorganized. It had been managed by a church elder from Georgia who had previously owned a photo studio. Naturally, he envisioned the photography department in terms that made sense to him. He could provide executive portraits but didn't think in terms of news photos. Nor was the department being run cost-effectively. John had seen some of the prints I had done doing lab work for Peter Simon back at B.U. and wanted some of that feel in the photos in the *Plain Truth*. He must have shown them to Dave Conn, the new department manager, who hired me as a lab assistant.

The rehabilitation meant that I could return to the *Portfolio*, again in the role, though not title, of managing editor. In the fall semester, Jeff Calkins was the editor, in the spring, Dennis Neill. The previous year, Keith and I had clicked immediately, and worked well in a synergetic re-lationship, while Mike, who became editor in the spring semester, and I had been friends ever since we arrived on campus. The relations with Jeff and Dennis were more difficult. Jeff had an extremely brilliant, incisive mind. I never asked him, but I'm sure one of his heroes was William F. Buckley, Jr. When he had made a particularly good point, he flashed the same grin of good-natured malice that Buckley had patented. We often differed over head-lines, layout, and many other details. The changeover to Dennis was a relief in one way, from nervous tension to high plateau cool. We spent a few weeks testing each other before settling into a working relationship that was both comfortable and productive.

I didn't last long in the Photography Department, but long enough to experience its move from the building it had shared with the TV studio (an old gun shop next to Ambassador Hall) to a building east of the main campus, now on the other side of the freeway construction. I no longer recall my infraction; I think it had to do with go-ing behind Dave's back on some matter that should have required his decision. Rather than simply reprimand me, Dave felt he had to let me go. A factor in his decision was that classes would soon resume, and I would drop back to a twenty-hour workweek. By laying me off, he could hire a recent graduate who was more certain to make photog-raphy his career. Dave correctly sensed the uncertainty about my future after graduation: writing, photography, or the field ministry? I retained my access to the lab to develop film and prints for each issue of the *Portfolio*.

My dismissal didn't lead to a repeat of my weeks'-long unemployment the previous year. Walking across campus just after being let go, I ran into Keith Oberlander, one of three brothers who worked for Ambassador. I gave an honest answer to his innocent, "How are you doing?" He listened and said I should not do anything for the moment. Before the day was out, I received word to see Michael Germano, dean of faculty.

When I went to see Germano, he hired me as the faculty aide to John Beaver, a young English professor. John was also the new faculty advisor of the *Portfolio*, in place of the person who had insisted I be fired from Editorial months earlier. As the faculty advisor, he was nominally responsible for the college's basic journalism course, but one of my duties, in addition to grading English exams, would be to teach that class. I still had my textbooks from B.U., borrowed a couple more from the Editorial Department, and embarked on my first experience of college teaching. Other fledgling teachers know what it's like to be one lesson preparation ahead of the class.

This was the second time I had gone to see Germano, who spearheaded the effort to upgrade Ambassador and gain accreditation. The previous time had been a year earlier when he had asked if I'd be interested in getting a master's degree in journalism. Germano saw a similar role for my friend Mike and sketched out a plan for which courses the two of us would take at the University of Southern California and what courses we would teach at Ambassador. The church would pay our tuition; we would continue to live on the Ambassador campus, where we already had room and board from our work-study program. We would have to take enough classes at Ambassador to continue our enrollment. He made similar arrangements with some other students with previous college degrees in other subject areas.

U.S.C. admitted me as a non-degree, special student, to begin in the spring semester 1972, with the requirement that I take one undergraduate course before taking graduate courses. On the recommendation of the department head, my status would then be changed to degree candidate, and up to twelve credits earned as a special student could be applied toward my degree. Germano asked me to delay my entry until fall 1972. Then, after being fired from Editorial in February, I forgot all about the arrangement. It came back to mind a couple of weeks after classes began in the fall. I found a letter from U.S.C. in my mailbox, saying that classes had begun, and I hadn't yet registered for any courses. I asked Germano what I should do. The academic budget had been cut, one of the effects of the decrease in income during Ted Armstrong's banishment, and the offer of having the college pay my grad school tuition was off the table. I wasn't averse to the idea of getting an additional degree, but I lacked a burning desire to do it. Otherwise, I'm sure I could have arranged a way to finance it.

Part of the philosophical struggle raging in Worldwide was the issue of whether to even seek accreditation for Ambassador. Was the college just to train workers for the Work—that is, augment Herbert Armstrong—or was it for providing a college education for all qualified youth in the church, even if many of them might not be employed by Worldwide after graduation? For this issue to even come up was a sign of time passing. When the college opened in 1947, it was a short twenty-five years to 1972. Now that we were still here, there were going to be more youths reaching college age—in some cases, children of original graduates—than the church could employ. Ted Armstrong railed on the broadcast that all the world's colleges were evil, only Ambassador was God's college. This led some to conclude that if they weren't accepted there, or if their area of interest was not an area on offer at Ambassador, then it was better to forego higher education than attend a worldly school. If the college broadened its mission to accommodate these, accreditation would be necessary.

Some were concerned, however, that the accreditors would demand a watering down or altering of distinctive teachings. Was this a tacit admission that some of what we taught wouldn't hold up under academic scrutiny? Perhaps. The example of what is now called Vanguard University shows that the fear was unfounded. It had been started as the Southern California Bible School by the Assemblies of God in 1920, and after adding a liberal arts program, had received accreditation in 1964 without compromising its church-related mission.

Ambassador's bid for accreditation had been rejected. The Western Association of Schools and Colleges put the candidacy on hold for three years to give the college time to address the shortcomings the association diagnosed. As it turned out, distinctive teachings didn't appear on their list. The biggest problem named in the report, alongside an undersized library, was governance. The association noted the interweaving of duties between the church, the college, and the media outreach. There was no independent board of trustees; almost all the board members at Ambassador not only had executive positions in the college, already unusual enough, but wore two or three other hats as well. This was a touchy subject for Herbert Armstrong, who insisted that God's government worked from the top down. In effect, that meant that Herbert Armstrong did not have to answer to any other human being.

The association noted as well that few faculty members had doctorates, and few had degrees from institutions other than Ambassador, which was why Germano had approached several of us with previous degrees to broach the idea of grad school.

Now, even though it looked as if I would not be attending U.S.C. to get a master's degree, I was teaching nevertheless. I found I enjoyed it, and I loved my job as managing editor of the school paper. The biggest challenge, given my poor finger dexterity, was the physical work of pasting the typed articles and headlines onto layout sheets. Life became much better when Wanda King joined the staff and did most of the paste-up. I also managed the photo staff, which had several talented individuals.

Soon after I returned to the *Portfolio*, our office moved from the space in the Editorial Department we'd occupied the previous year to a study area in the Grove Terrace dorm. Since the *Portfolio* was a student publication, this was a more appropriate location for us.

Jeff had one desk cubicle, next to the sliding door leading to the east-facing balcony. When Dennis became editor in the spring semester, that became his cubicle. I had the cubicle on the other side so that we worked back to back. The IBM Selectric we used to compose text was in a cubicle just inside of the hallway door, the Varityper opposite it. The other four cubicles could be used by other staff members to type their stories, although one was semi-permanently occupied by Larry Gott.

Larry was a grandson of Herbert Armstrong, with a round face that bore more than a passing resemblance to his grandfather's. Larry was nearly thirty and was "between opportunities." He wanted to return to school but didn't have any money. His grandfather offered to pick up his tuition, but only if he came to Ambassador. Larry had spent his entire life around the church. His mother, Beverly, was still a member when he was a child, then she was disfellowshipped. The reason given to the membership was that she refused to stop wearing make-up during one of her father's periodic crackdowns. So, to Larry, Herbert Armstrong was not "God's Apostle," as the rest of us viewed him, but Grandpa, both dispenser and withholder of benefits.

Larry sensed that his grandfather's hope was that he would finally become a member of Worldwide. He proudly wore his non-member status and was suspicious of any fellow student, male or female, who tried to become friends. He suspected the administration had told them to "be nice" to him in the hopes of his conversion. He may have been right. He was a good writer and was a valuable addition to the *Portfolio* staff. His byline even appeared in the *Plain Truth*, which was highly unusual for a student. But not all the time he spent in his cubicle in our newsroom was spent writing. More than one night, I sat up late with him to listen to lamentations fueled by what may have been one beer too many. At other times, we played chess, which had become popular on campus when Bobby Fischer arrived after his victory in Reykjavik. In later years, whenever someone asked how well I played, I could boast that I had lost to someone (Larry) who had lost to someone (Robert Kuhn) who had lost to Fischer.

Larry produced a reliable stream of entertaining copy, but to me, his greatest service was his presence in the office the one time his grandfather telephoned, irate that we had refused to run an article by his son, Ted.

Ted Armstrong was out of town to meet with station executives and appear on radio call-in programs. Unexpectedly, he sent a report on his trip for us to run in the *Portfolio*, but it arrived the day after we had sent that week's issue to press. After my experience the year before, I was not about to run down to the press and yell, "stop the presses!" What I did do stupider. Dave Albert was away and had asked me to substitute for him in his Epistles of Paul class. I had prepared a lesson showing how Paul's ministry was conventionally divided into three missionary journeys. Ted Armstrong's letter had arrived just before I left for class and, after finishing my lesson, the hour having nearly expired, I read his letter at breakneck speed to the class, who may have felt like hostages at that point.

That didn't make Ted Armstrong feel any better over having missed our deadline, which had prevented us from running his article while it was timely. He complained to his father, and his father called us. Larry was there to take the call, thereby earning my eternal gratitude. He assured his Grandpa he would look into it and find out what happened, assuaging the wrath. He then reported that the article had indeed arrived after our deadline. What Larry knew from experience, but I didn't, was that these storms generally passed as quickly as they arose.

Senior year meant service opportunities, as well. We couldn't help reading these as others might read tea leaves to foresee how the administration viewed our potential usefulness to the Work. After finishing my junior year as treasurer of my Ambassador Club, I hoped to be a club president in my senior year but was disappointed to learn I would be a vice-president instead. That was balanced out, though, by becoming a campus tour guide. I enjoyed this opportunity to be the first public face for visitors to the campus. They included prospective college students with skeptical parents, church members from all over the world, and locals curious to learn more about the college that had revitalized the decaying west end of Pasadena and repeatedly won awards for the most beautifully-landscaped campus in Southern California.

In my senior year, there was an increased emphasis on the Bible in my course load. George Kemnitz had been brought in from the field ministry to Pasadena to offer a ministerial-preparation concentration as well as a program for ministers in from the field.

In addition to Comparative Religion (fourth-year Bible), which Kemnitz taught, and the Epistles of Paul (now taught by Dave Albert in place of Ron Dart), I also was accepted to Kemnitz's one-semester General Epistles course. Participants were a mix of seniors and ministers brought in for a sabbatical. Among them was John, my mentor from

New England. It was the only course I had in Pasadena taught seminar-style. For each meeting, one of us had to prepare an exegetical paper that we presented orally. To me, it was the best course I had at Ambassador.

A second, competing vision of ministerial preparation came in the person of Raymond Cole, one of the original four students when the college opened in 1947, one of the first five evangelists ordained in 1952. Cole and his brother Wayne had been teenagers in Oregon when Herbert Armstrong spoke in congregations there before his relocation to Pasadena. After graduation from college, Raymond Cole had preceded Rod Meredith as the first superintendent of ministers.

Now, twenty years later, after serving as pastor to numerous congregations and district superintendent, then supervising the construction of feast sites in the Poconos and Wisconsin Dells, he had been brought back to Pasadena. There was talk that his ultra-conservative ways had something to do with it, but his duties as assistant to Dave Antion, current director of Church Administration (as the job of superintendent of ministers was now called) included serving as an advisor to senior class students, particularly those who might be destined for the field ministry. He had given the sermon the first time I attended Worldwide services in the summer of 1967 and had rendered judgment in the question of whether I had to break my engagement to be baptized. He decreed no; it was up to my fiancée to decide what to do if I should enter the church. I was inclined to respect him, but the more I heard some of my classmates swoon over his advice, the more skeptical I became. Cole was strict with himself. He slept four hours a night and drove himself during his working hours, despite suffering from migraines. I felt it was his business how he spent his time, but he encouraged the students around him to do the same things, which I didn't care for.

George Kemnitz and Raymond Cole seemed to personify for me a conflict that had been palpable from the time I arrived in Pasadena, but now, in the spring of 1973, seemed to sharpen. At the time, it seemed to be a struggle between liberal and conservative forces.

That may have been an accurate portrayal if viewed in the context of the hermetic world of Ambassador College. If seen in the light of the spectrum of Christianity, it was more accurately "mildly fundamentalist" versus "extreme fundamentalist." We students were torn. My way of coping was to read and reread Paul's Epistle to the Romans. I found comfort, especially from the second chapter, which contains Paul's analysis of how both observant Jews and non-Jews ("Gentiles") had missed the point. "All have sinned, and come short of the glory of God" (Rom. 3:23) was one of many verses I underlined and highlighted with red pencil. To me, this applied as well to the stricter and less-strict sides in the Church's own little tug-of-war. The point all had missed, Paul was telling me, was grace in Christ, "the righteousness of God without the law" (Rom. 3:21).

A little while previously, I had retrieved from a dumpster an old binder of reprint letters sent out in answer to letters from subscribers. The binder also included a letter Herbert Armstrong had written to those who handled the correspondence more than ten years earlier. He was on a fasting retreat in Palm Springs, and while reviewing outgoing letters detected a tendency to emphasize obedience to God's law and neglect of mention that the basis of salvation was faith in Christ. That gave me the courage to believe I wasn't totally misinterpreting Paul. I was slowly beginning to form my own opinions about Worldwide based on my own reading of the Bible.

The final year of speech was called Homiletics and Pastoral Administration. We were finally allowed to prepare sermonettes. This wasn't pure joy, however. I had regressed in speaking since my first year, something not only I noticed, but also something my friend Randy commented on. The lowest point was the assignment to explain a point of doctrine. I had no idea what to speak on. My speech lab was first class after lunch. My last class before lunch had been Epistles, and I thought one of the scriptures Dave Albert explained would be a good topic, so I quickly put together a speech based on that. As luck would have it, our regular lab instructor couldn't come. Who was substituting? None other than Dave Albert.

It's hard to give a speech when you're feeling mortified; there was more squirming as he worked me over afterward.

It was one of my most embarrassing moments in college, but there was a coda. Shortly before leaving Pasadena, a date and I went to dinner with Dave and his wife. He expressed regret that I couldn't stay and get an advanced degree in theology and join the faculty. But he knew it wasn't realistic. Theology courses were assigned to those with established reputations in the church.

Unalloyed joy was a course in Basic Musicianship (sight-reading and ear training) Gary Prather introduced that year to upgrade the skills of chorale members. The only wrinkle: it was offered at the same time as Lucy Martin's Music Appreciation course. Herbert Armstrong had declared her course an inviolable graduation requirement back in the day when most incoming students had little exposure to classical music. He felt they needed this polish before being sent to the field as ministers. Most students took it in their first year, but I had put it off.

I went to see Lucy Martin, a slim, elegant woman who had headed the Music Department since the college's inception. At first, she categorically refused. No one had ever been excused from her class. Only my insistence that I would have gladly taken it, but that I would be taking another music course in its place led her to relent enough to say that she would be willing to consider it if I could pass the final exam then and there, with no time for preparation. I agreed. I received the dispensation, but Mrs. Martin didn't tell me the grade. The department secretary who graded it revealed to me that I had aced it—a senior year bookend to the experience of taking two language exams in orientation week in the time allotted for one and getting the top score in both.

Testing out of the class wasn't a matter of getting away with something. Herbert Armstrong's goal was that each student learn to appreciate music, and in my case, there was very little I appreciated more. Whether performing in the Feast fun show—that year, I sang "(Take Me Home) Country Roads" with Marc Stahl's elegant guitar accompaniment and two coeds harmonizing on the chorus—or singing with the chorale in services and concerts, music continued to be an important part of my life. In addition to performing music, I also enjoyed listening to live music, including a revival of *Oliver* at the Hollywood Bowl with Ron Moody and Davey Jones reprising their original roles, a concert conducted by Aaron Copland, and John Stewart, formerly of the Kingston Trio, at Pasadena's finest coffee house, the Ice House.

Chapter Ten

That fall celebration of the Feast of Tabernacles was my fourth, and my third at Squaw Valley as a student. As in previous years, the students left the day after Atonement and stopped at Yosemite. For two years, I had been content in the basic amenities of the two-bed wooden cabins; this time, a classmate suggested we splurge and share a room at the Ahwahnee Inn, an enjoyable taste of luxury. As if to atone for it, I had to share a single bed in the athletes' dorms at Squaw Valley. Herbert Armstrong had returned from Japan just before the school year started and brought the son of one of his Japanese connections for a year of college. Rooms for the feast had already been booked; there was nothing available for him unless he shared a bed. My friend Randy, as student body president, was charged with solving the problem and asked me. He told me to look at the request as a measure of his estimate of the depth of my conversion.

We also had an Indian princess in the student body that year, the niece of one of the dignitaries who had befriended Herbert Armstrong on his tours. She came to the feast as well, and she was my date for dinner at the Ahwahnee that year. It turned out the Maharishi Mahesh Yogi, of Beatle and Transcendental Meditation fame, was spending a few days at Lake Tahoe as well. As I understood it, protocol obliged the princess to render him a visit. She took two coeds with her, one of them, my good friend Margie.

My mentor John, was also in Squaw Valley, offered to let me use his fleet car one evening in case there were anyone special I wanted to take out. I leapt at the opportunity, so after the second service one day, I drove his car out of the parking lot.

In addition to blanketing the airwaves and having a large circulation magazine, the church was built on gasoline and tire rubber. Interested readers asked for contact with a "local representative," as they were called in our literature. So, ministers spent much of each workweek on the road, racking up sixty thousand miles a year and more. It was cheaper for the church to operate a fleet program and have the ministers drive late-model, full- or mid-size cars than to pay the ministry enough for them to afford to buy their own cars and replace them every two or three years.

At the feast, ministers had parking spaces closer to the

meeting hall—a nice perk. To help traffic monitors guide them to the right lot, ministers were given special bumper stickers. While all the other members had green stickers, theirs were orange.

What I experienced when I drove out of the parking lot that afternoon and returned the next morning was like the movie scenes in which obsequious bellboys nearly bow in half as they say "right this way, sir" to illustrious guests. What the parking monitors thought or muttered under their breath as a skinny, twenty-four-year-old whippersnapper at the wheel drove by is something I'd rather not know.

I felt out of place, a fraud, but I also enjoyed the treatment.

Herbert Armstrong, from the time the college turned out its first graduates, had understood the difficulty of sending young men to found congregations to serve people interested in Armstrong's radio ministry. It's no surprise that these young men didn't always receive the respect Herbert Armstrong felt a minister of Christ should receive as they expounded the will of God to farmers, grizzled war veterans, and others who knew a thing or two about life. Armstrong insisted members address the ministers as "Mister" with their last names and set a dress code for the ministry—business suit and tie, carrying hard-shell briefcases. Along with the voice personality he encouraged them to develop, these were the external trappings of authority. The fleet car was one more expression of this.

The feast 1972 also was the first time the revised church hymnal was used. The previous hymnal had been a saddle-stitched softcover, like a thick booklet. Alongside hymns by Herbert Armstrong's brother, Dwight (settings of old rhymed Psalm paraphrases), there were some popular Protestant standards, some with words modified to reflect Worldwide's teachings. It was no secret that Herbert Armstrong hadn't cared for them and kept his brother on salary to produce more of his own. Now, after delays, the new book was ready; it was hardbound in the Ambassador colors, purple and gold. I had a private preview the evening before Atonement. One of the coeds who accompanied services had an advance copy and invited me to share her piano bench in the Fine Arts Hall as she went through the book and practiced her sight-reading on the new ones. To me, they included some of Dwight Armstrong's more successful settings.

The hymnal filled with the church's own hymns was one of the distinctive features of being part of Worldwide. Some were better than others. Dwight Armstrong's setting of Psalm 51, "In thy loving kindness, Lord," since it was about repentance, often featured in services. I could never shake the feeling, however, that the melody sounded more like one that should be played by a brass band marching down a football field.

A month after the feast, we had an unusual sing-along. We were used to having these unscheduled events announced spontaneously. This one would be held in the gym rather than the student center, where they normally were. The reason: Merle Haggard would perform. Ted Armstrong had a big following among truckers and others who were on the road late at night. This included many country singers. Many had been raised as church-goers, but life on the road meant little time for church. Besides, that life could make them feel like outsiders in a typical, respectable setting.

Ted Armstrong first met Haggard while both were boating on Lake Havasu and soon discovered they were mutual fans. Haggard asked a favor: It was often difficult to find the *World Tomorrow* when they were scanning for it on the radio of their tour bus. Would it be possible to have tapes sent? Armstrong said he'd be glad to if, in return, Haggard would perform at the college.

During the day, we heard what was in store for us that night. The gym was transformed by truckloads of hay bales brought in for seating. The first half was the usual sing-a-long format, with Ted Armstrong, flanked by his son Mark, Jim Thornhill, and Randal Dick, leading in songs from our student-produced sing-a-long book. Then Haggard took the stage, backed by his crack touring band, the Strangers. They ran through "Silver Wings," "Today, I Started Loving You Again," and other hits. Sammi Smith, touring with them, sang her cover of "Help Me Make It Through the Night," which topped the country charts at the time.

Word filtered back from Haggard's team: the night before, at a concert somewhere in central California, Haggard had been as depressed as his crew had ever seen him. They wondered how he would take to showing up at a small college to repay a debt with a free concert. It turned out that he was more uplifted that night than they had seen him in a long time.

The day after the concert, we received a request from Ted Armstrong's office: rather than report the concert in a normal issue of the *Portfolio*, could we put out a special edition that he could send to Haggard? So, we produced two papers that week. I had access to photos that the church's full-time photographers had taken, but also included several of my own, including a close-up filling the front page. It was satisfying to have the other photographers notice the difference between my photos and theirs. Their training had taught them to add light to get sharper images. My training had been to use natural light wherever possible. Experience from photographing in clubs and theaters in Boston had taught me that the spotlights provided plenty of light. Were I to supplement that with flash, it would remove the drama from the photo. The result would be very different from what the audience had seen.

Life on campus returned to normal. The rising hulk of the auditorium on the east side of the main plaza was a constant presence that I passed every time I walked be-

tween the student center and the administration building during my senior year. From just about anywhere on
campus, one could see the 150-foot crane. Some asked why
a college with a student body of 550 needed a 1200-seat
auditorium, but having worked so often on set-up and
take-down crews Friday afternoon and Saturday evening
to transform the gym into the college chapel, I didn't ask.
I knew it would fill for Bible study and services on the
weekend. Since I hadn't been on campus in the Fifties and
Sixties, when each project had been done on a shoestring,
I had no context to realize that this was something new.
Whenever Herbert Armstrong returned from one of his
overseas trips, he boasted of the marble he had ordered
here or the onyx there, or the crystal chandeliers; no expense was spared. Nor did I connect the expense with the
layoffs and cutbacks being made in other departments. It
was simply exciting to see it going up.

Meanwhile, the income of the church stagnated. The
biggest lag was in the building fund. Some members had
no more to give, others failed to see why they should sacrifice for distant luxury. Meanwhile, my feeling continued
to be, if it's for God, why not the best?

In January, Larry came to the office and told me to
grab my camera. He took me in hand, and we tagged along
as his grandfather gave ministers in town for that year's
conference a tour of the construction site. The budget dictated that only district superintendents from the U. S. and

Canada, college officials, and international office managers attend that year. A few of them looked at me strangely, as if wondering why someone they didn't know was there, but I continued clicking away. This confirmed something I had experienced before: if you have a good camera and act like you belong there, people generally let you get on with your business.

Still, it was another of the situations I wouldn't have been in if Larry didn't take me along. Another was that I was present in the recital hall of the Fine Arts building when Lucy Martin took delivery of the two matching Steinways from Hamburg (those built in New York wouldn't have been good enough) for the auditorium. It's also how I got aboard the Gulfstream for a tour once when Herbert Armstrong landed from one of his trips.

The auditorium tour also gave me a chance to observe the interaction of these men (a few wives were there as well). One stood out particularly: Raymond McNair's dogged attempts to amuse Herbert Armstrong with his corny jokes, and the look of contempt that crossed Armstrong's face in an unguarded moment. From then on, I couldn't shake the feeling that he felt McNair was a buffoon, but a loyal, useful one.

A tradition in the senior year was an invitation to dine with Herbert Armstrong in his home, officially known as the campus social center. It was a strictly formal occasion, gowns for the coeds, dinner jacket and black tie for the men. The dinners took place throughout the year, with groups of twelve taking part. First, Armstrong showed us around the home.

After a while, I had a hard time keeping straight which of the ornaments had once belonged to the Tsarina and which had been gifts from William Randolph Hearst to Marion Davies. Then we sat in the living room and chatted stiffly over a glass of sherry. At one point, Armstrong went to the baby grand in the corner and played the first movement of Beethoven's "Moonlight" Sonata. When dinner was served, we proceeded to the table, set with full dinner service and gold cutlery. Armstrong raised a glass and toasted "to the many happy hours I spent in the arms of another man's wife . . . My mother!"

I ended up going twice. I had already had my turn, but one evening, just as we gathered in the student center for our evening meal, we heard an announcement that one student scheduled for that evening was ill and they needed a replacement right away. A couple of minutes passed, and no one volunteered, so I agreed to go. I hurried back to my dorm and changed, affixing cufflinks to the French cuffs of my formal shirt (thankfully clean and ironed). As I joined the group gathered outside Armstrong's home, and they learned I had been there before, some of the women said they would depend on me to carry the conversation. Unfortunately, I tried to comply, and after one of my jokes, the same look crossed Herbert Armstrong's face that I had seen him give Raymond McNair during the tour of the Auditorium building site.

The rationale for these dinners was that we would soon be representing the church, and Armstrong wanted us to be able to conduct ourselves well in any circumstances we might find ourselves in. If some of us got the idea that we were expected to copy this lifestyle, so much the worse for us. At the time, I didn't agree with those who complained about Armstrong's extravagance. Since I accepted his claim that he was God's end time messenger, nothing could be too good for him, could it?

One late January weekend, the chorale and band boarded buses early on a Friday morning and headed north to the Bay Area. We were to sing for a combined service of the San Francisco and Oakland congregations and provide entertainment at a social on Saturday night. It was my first visit to a city that held fond memories for my dad as the port of arrival when he returned from service in the Pacific in 1945. My memory of my first visit there is less fond. I fell ill with the flu and spent the weekend in bed. The odor of stale cigar smoke in the linen added to my discomfort.

A more pleasant memory is of a production of the *Pirates of Penzance*, which the chorale staged at the San Gabriel Civic Auditorium. Gary Prather had mounted some musicals before, but with the limitation that they be concert performances. But now he thought the time might be right to risk a costumed, staged, made-up production, despite

Herbert Armstrong's aversion to play-acting. Prather's ace in the hole was that Mr. Armstrong's grandson, Larry, would make the very model of a modern major general. Prather cast the other solo roles, including me, as the pirate lieutenant Samuel. Prather had been right: Herbert Armstrong sat in the middle of the front row and beamed.

In the middle of the spring semester, shortly after Ted Armstrong further consolidated his administrative control by becoming executive manager of operations. Meredith and Raymond McNair, deputy chancellor of the Bricket Wood campus, traded jobs; Meredith had been deputy chancellor in Pasadena for one-and-a-half semesters. The deputy chancellor of Big Sandy, Les McCullough, and the director of Worldwide's international activities, Ron Dart, swapped as well.

McNair lasted only three months in his new role. At the end of the semester, the office of deputy chancellor in Pasadena was eliminated. It had only been created less than a year-and-a-half earlier, during Ted Armstrong's banishment, but in that short time, had been filled by three. Now Ted Armstrong, who had become president of the college with Herbert Armstrong remaining chairman of the board of trustees, interacted directly with Michael Germano. Germano had been Vice-President of Academic Affairs (Dean of Faculty) now became Executive Vice-President, with oversight of the college on a day-to-day basis.

As had happened in my junior year, my senior year

brought a shuffle of instructors in the Bible courses, this time not at semester break, but mid-way through the spring semester. Dave Antion streamlined the organization of the field ministry. The twelve districts were rearranged into eight regions, which he hoped would enable him to interact on a more continuous basis with the superintendents, now renamed regional directors. He also brought fresh blood into the ranks. The superintendents had tended to be the longest-serving ministers. Antion wanted to change this based on a job profile and skill assessment. To aid in the process, he called in a management consultant to interview and evaluate the candidates. Antion didn't get all of his first choices for the eight positions approved, but enough of them that he was satisfied with the results.

One of them was George Kemnitz, who packed up on short notice for Chicago. The fact that we were two months from graduation made no difference. Dave Albert, who had taken over the Epistles of Paul class that year from Ron Dart, now switched to fourth-year Bible, Comparative Religion, and Al Carrozzo was catapulted into Albert's class. This was done on short notice, and all Carrozzo could do with the class was to treat it as he would a Bible study in a local church area, reading verse by verse, interspersed with the church's idiosyncratic interpretations written in the margins of his Bible.

Dave Albert would have preferred to continue teaching the class he had prepared to teach, but adapted to the shuffle more ably than Carrozzo, quickly getting up to speed on the topics. Once again, he asked me to do an in-class presentation. He had been talking with some of us outside of class about the run-away success of Hal Lindsey's book, *The Late Great Planet Earth*. In it, Lindsey made a case for the imminent return of Jesus Christ, using many of the same numerical calculations based on Daniel and Revelation that we did. He also made several of the same correlations of current nations with Bible figures, such as a united Europe as the Beast of Revelation. Worldwide had been broadcasting this for decades, with a measure of success, but had not attained the mainstream awareness that Lindsey had. Albert asked three of us to research end-time views among Protestants and use one class period to report on what we found.

We also had a change in faculty advisor for the *Portfolio* in the wake of another shake-up in Editorial. *Tomorrow's World*, the magazine slotted between the widely-circulated *Plain Truth* and the members-only *Good News*, was canceled, the *Plain Truth* was to revert to more overtly religious content, and Paul Kroll, who had been functioning as managing editor—without the title—was out. He now brought his high energy level to the *Portfolio*, quite a change from the laid-back, hands-off approach of John Beaver. He instituted weekly meetings for the entire staff, Sunday evening at five, and took a desk in our office in Grove Terrace.

He analyzed every stage of production from assignment to circulating the printed results to improve quality and efficiency. He also yearned to make the paper more relevant and was not shy about courting controversy in the process. When Deputy Chancellor McNair hosted the faculty in his home near the end of the semester, for instance, Paul wrote about it in the Portfolio, noting the poignancy that for many, it was a farewell gathering, given the latest round of budget cuts.

In mid-March, Dennis and I met with Ted Armstrong in his office away from the office. In spite of his new range of executive responsibility, he hardly set foot on the fourth floor of the Hall of Administration. Instead, he used a small room at the television building, sharing it with Robert Kuhn and Jim Thornhill. Executives cooled their heels in a small anteroom while waiting their turn.

Dennis had asked for the meeting to discuss *Portfolio* matters with him, including some letters we had received from members asking if they could receive the paper to be better informed of what was going on at headquarters. It turned out the meeting was fortuitous from Ted Armstrong's point of view; he was forging plans for a church newspaper. He aimed to recapture the spirit of the early days when members formed a close-knit flock. The letters we had received would bolster his argument when he sought his father's approval for the project. The first issue of the *Worldwide News* appeared a month later, produced by John Robinson's team in Big Sandy, but with two of my articles on the front page.

I returned another time to the television building that spring. Ted Armstrong planned a series of four programs about Ambassador College. One of the programs would include students talking about why they came to Ambassador. I was one of those invited to a roundtable discussion to generate the soundtrack. A film crew then filmed us as we sat in a classroom as if listening to a lecture. Something went wrong with the sound recording, so a few months later, after I left the campus, a student told me he had to record my remarks, so in the finished program, it was his voice over my picture.

I had one other brush with media fame. The church encouraged involvement among its listeners by offering, in addition to subscriptions to the *Plain Truth*, booklets on various topics of interest, both religious and social. Now that Ted Armstrong was doing a daily telecast as well, our booklet program was being revamped, both editorially and graphically. One of his recurrent themes was the sexual revolution, so he ordered an update of our booklet on dating. The cover of the original edition featured a pleasant but outdated watercolor of a couple walking side by side. One of the church's photographers, Dave Verrell, was commissioned to create a new cover. He cast me and another senior, Jill, as his models. Jill was a southern Californian who had spent her first three years in Big Sandy, transferring to Pasadena for her senior year. Dave drove us up into the San Gabriel Mountains late one afternoon with Jill and I sitting in the flatbed of his pickup truck. She was also in the chorale, so we sang on the way up and back. Rattling around in the pickup truck brought to mind a song she hadn't heard before, Woody Guthrie's "Plane Wreck at Los Gatos (Deportees)," which I sang for her.

Dave found a good location and took a series of photos of us as the sun set. Apparently, his photos turned out too well. A few weeks later, I heard that some of the higher-ups thought them "too romantic" and nixed them. Unfortunately, I never saw any of the photos.

Spring semester senior year was also the time when students were permitted to date "pursuant to marriage," as it was put. For some, the process seemed to go smoothly, the natural outcome of years of being together in classes and on activities. But not for me. There were several girls who were good friends, first among them Margie, but she had graduated, so I saw less of her. There were two or three others I dated often with vague notions that one of them might be "the one." As the semester got underway, I began seeing more of them, a junior, Kathy, a blonde from the Midwest with sparkling blue-eyes, dimpled cheeks, and an infectious smile.

The senior trip was looming. This was financed each year by proceeds from the Rose Bowl. This year we had invested a great deal of work and planning; a junior with a flair for management walked us through it. Parking, concessions, programs, as well as the rental from the stands we put up on church property lining the route, brought in good proceeds.

The trip was well-planned, too. We went up the Pacific Coast Highway, with stops at Solvang and Hearst's San Simeon, an overnight in San Francisco and a day sight-seeing there (much more pleasant than my first visit), then—with several stops for wine-tasting along the way—Squaw Valley for skiing. The trip was for the entire senior class, but any senior in a committed relationship with a junior could invite him or her along. Things had not reached that point in my friendship, though. I was torn by self-doubt and was loath to commit. I did buy Kathy a present as a souvenir of the trip, and soon after returning, we grew closer and felt we had an understanding, sealed with a kiss in a secluded garden at a corner of the campus.

The next morning, after sleeping poorly, I was in turmoil. I spent a long time in a prayer closet but didn't feel that my prayers rose any higher than the ceiling. I was afraid I was making a mistake and shared my feelings with Kathy when we met at breakfast. I made an appointment with a counselor in the dean's office and arrived to find I got there just after she finished talking with the same counselor. I heard an earful. One thing stuck. He didn't repeat everything she had said, but he did ask me about my mother and about my relationship with her. Apparently,

Kathy had shared with him that it struck her that I never mentioned her. I often spoke of my father, but my silence about my mom left her wondering if she were dead. I'm grateful to her that she was the first one to put her finger on that problem and verbalize it. If not directly to me, at least in a way that got back to me. I began to realize that, in addition to the uncertainty over what I would do after graduation, this was a factor in my difficulty in committing.

As fate would have it, there was a sing-a-long that night, the one in which the revised songbook Randal Dick and I had put so much effort into preparing, was introduced. Randy was on stage, along with Ted Armstrong and the others. Randy had difficulty matching his vocal to one of the new songs, though, stopped and called out, "Where's Henry?" Finally, the summons I was waiting for to join the band at the front. I had been in front before on occasion for special numbers, but this was the first time I was asked to join the lineup alongside Ted Armstrong and the others. It couldn't have come at a worse time, though. Before the first song was finished, I caught sight of my now-ex walking out the back.

My memory of the last sing-a-long before leaving college is more pleasant. It's only natural for seniors to want to let it all hang-out just before graduation. In my case, that also expressed itself in music. I was sitting on a bench in front of a dorm, quietly playing my guitar when Sam, a fellow senior, asked if I knew "The Weight" by the Band. It turned out that our taste in music was similar. He suggested putting a combo together and working up that song and Dylan's "I Shall Be Released" for the last sing-a-long before graduation. We rehearsed for hours in the college band room until we had both songs down tight, so tight that we could play loosely. Student contributions were a time for the sing-a-long team to leave the stage, take a break and get a beer, but as we played—nervous as to how this foray into rock music would go over—we noticed Ted Armstrong turn in the far corner and watch us intently, beer in hand. We didn't sense disapproval in his face.

Senior year is a weighty time at all colleges and universities, but the spring semester of senior year at Ambassador College was more so. Since the purpose of the college was to train manpower for the needs of the church, job assignments were made. Although I had taken the courses that were part of the ministerial preparation concentration, that was no guarantee that I would be sent to the field, nor even of full-time employment after graduation. The college had grown to the point where not all graduates could be absorbed into the work.

In the early spring, just days after I had broken up with Kathy, David Antion called thirteen seniors into his office. I was slotted for the eleventh appointment. The ten students before me, including my good friend Randy, had been told they would be sent to the field; there would be eleven assignments in all as trainees in the U.S. I arrived for my appointment, ready for anything except what awaited me, Antion's question: "Henry, what do you want to do?" He went on to say that it was not clear whether I wanted to be in the ministry or to work in journalism. I was flummoxed but answered that I hadn't come to Ambassador to pursue what I wanted to do but to help the Work in whatever way was best.

There were no specifics discussed, certainly not what the alternatives in journalism might be. Instead, the conversation grew stranger. Antion brought up the fact that I was twenty-five years old. "You'd better hurry up," he added, "I was ordained an evangelist when I was thirty." I had no idea how to process that remark and left the office mildly shocked. The next two students had their interviews and were also told they might be sent to the field, that there was one remaining slot and three candidates. One of them went across the hall on the fourth floor of the Hall of Administration building to the International Office, made an appointment with Ron Dart, and before the end of the day, had an assignment in Canada as a ministerial trainee. So that left two of us.

A "maybe" in the field. I felt as if this were God's general evaluation of me. A maybe. Once again, I berated myself for my double-mindedness, using the Bible term from James 1:8 for an indecisive, easily-distracted person. It came out in my romances and now in my work goals. I had no idea what else I would do if I were not employed by Worldwide in some way. I was reluctant to return to New Jersey and go to work for my father in his delicatessen. I hadn't been the prodigal son—I had left home not to squander my inheritance, but to obey the will of God. It would have been not only embarrassing but also ironic if, after these years in Pasadena, I returned home.

This was all in the weeks before the Passover, the time of intensive self-examination. Worldwide denounced Lent, the forty days of fasting and self-examination before Easter, as pagan, based on old myths about Osiris or Tammuz. The irony was that since we only celebrated the Lord's Supper once a year, on the anniversary of its institution in the Gospels (our Passover), we prepared for it as scrupulously as the most fervent Catholic. It didn't seem coincidental to me that the fallout from the love-in during my first year in Pasadena, or the humiliating weeks of being the only student without a job in my second year had come at this time. Nor that this time of uncertainty while waiting to see what, if anything, God wanted me to do in the Work would happen now.

Mike suggested we spend a long weekend at Lake Arrowhead. We rented a room in an inexpensive inn. I used one of the days to fast. Mike, battling health issues, didn't. We read the Bible, hiked, talked.

Soon after, the other candidate was told he would be going as the eleventh trainee. I was told nothing.

What I didn't know was that Editorial was seeking to beef up its presence in Europe. The *Plain Truth* staff was centered in Pasadena. There were also contributions from employees in various regional offices of the church. For over a year, the magazine had also had two correspondents, Dexter Faulkner in Washington, D.C., and Ray Kosanke (the former Stanford All-American who had anchored the senior basketball team in my first year in Pasadena) in Brussels. Editorial hoped for more reporting from Europe, however, than they were receiving. There were a handful of talented journalists in the senior class, Dennis, Jeff, and, in my opinion, the best of us all, Mike. But I was the only one who spoke German and French. Roger Lippross, the production coordinator for the magazine, arranged for a job interview with Wayne Cole, now head of the Publishing Division, responsible for both the Press and Editorial. Lippross arranged it for a time when Charles Hunting, without whose approval nothing happened, not only in the British Isles but also on the European continent, was in Pasadena and would happen to be in Lippross's office.

So, after the stress of being a maybe, then having no prospect of employment, I received a surprising dream assignment: foreign correspondent. When I left the Hall of Administration that day, I was probably the most elated person on campus. A vague goal that first formed when I was fourteen and read William Shirer's *Berlin Diary* in the summer between eighth and ninth grade. It was the

reason I had used my early fulfillment of science require-
ments to take French in addition to German in high school.
I would be returning to Brussels, still a clear memory from
the day and night spent there with my aunt and uncle and
my cousins when we had toured Europe nine years earlier.
I remembered the haunting strains of the oriental song I
had heard from an open window while we walked narrow
streets in search of the Grand Place and the fragrance of
chicory mixed with the brewing coffee that wafted out
from those windows.

Progress in European integration had not kept pace
with our prophetic timetable and seemed to lag behind
developments in the Middle East. But in January 1973, the
European Community expanded from six to nine members, including Great Britain. That was getting close to the
ten we understood the Book of Revelation to call for. And
at the summit meeting in late 1972 to prepare for welcoming the new members, the representatives of the nine nations drew up an ambitious timetable, culminating in full
unification in 1980.

Visitors to the Ambassador campus that spring included two Germans, Klaus Mehnert, a journalist with a
specialty in foreign affairs, and Karl Günther Renz, the
presenter of the evening news (*Heute*) on one of the two
German networks, ZDF. They each spoke at an assembly,
and I was one of a few students invited to meet them in a
smaller setting, along with members of the editorial and

television departments.

I was still euphoric about moving to Europe when Frank Schnee, director of the German work in for a year of college, took the stage during the announcement period of the last day of Unleavened Bread to announce that there had been an auto accident on the way to services in Germany. All four passengers died. Two were secretaries from the church's Düsseldorf office, one was a student from Bricket Wood, and the fourth a prospective member. Despite the fate of Dick Armstrong, such occurrences were rare enough to be shocking. Why would God allow something so tragic on the way to observing one of his festivals?

Much less somber in the overall picture, but wistful for me personally was that after two-and-a-half years with the most eligible young women in the church, it seemed I would graduate unattached. My mentor John, thinking of my career, urged me to court the daughter of one the original evangelists; I admired her but felt no romantic spark—nor did I sense any interest on her part. The coed I had taken on that special night out during the feast and had dated often that year began to show interest, but then I rushed the question of whether she'd consider marrying me at graduation; she wisely refused. She was one of the most avidly courted women in our class; I was the latest in her series of intriguing possibilities, but nothing more. Another, a graduate who was my age, gave me an affectionate kiss on the cheek and promised to visit me in Europe. And when Margie, the Imperial teacher I had been involved with the previous year, and I said our farewells, she told me: "Don't misunderstand what I'm about to say. I don't want to pressure you, but I do love you."

Chapter Eleven

My two years and nine months in Southern California ended in a sprint: the final sing-along, grad ball, the outdoor graduation ceremony in the sunken gardens down the hill from the library; then, it was over. A photo of me taken after the ceremony appeared in the next year's yearbook, the *Envoy*. My smiling mouth is open so wide it's a wonder my jaw didn't become unhinged.

In the few remaining days in Pasadena, I sold the stereo system I had bought second-hand from another graduate two years earlier and packed my books and other belongings in a few boxes. I took them, along with my Framus guitar, to the college's Shipping and Receiving Department to be put into a container taking the Schnees' household back to Europe. Paul and Connie, two of our gang of four in German III—both hired to work in Germany—did the same.

I was in a hurry to go over, eager to begin working in the heart of Europe, at the center of what we believed was the nascent beast power, the ten-nation consortium that would be the last revival of the Holy Roman Empire (Rev. 13:1), but I stopped over in New Jersey for a short stay, a little less than three weeks. My classmate Mike came with me, on his way to dig in Jerusalem. We used the one day before his continuing flight to go into the city, where we visited the *New York Times*. Mike got us into the office suite James Reston shared with Mike's fellow North Carolinian and distant kin Tom Wicker. Neither gentleman was in, but we had a friendly chat with their secretary.

My time home was brief but long enough for another romance. Angie, a young woman from a neighboring town, was home for the summer between her sophomore and junior years at Ambassador Big Sandy. I hadn't met her or her sisters on any of my previous visits to the local congregation, but now we saw each other at services and Bible study. I asked her out to the movies. Bob Dylan had a role in a new western by Sam Peckinpah and had contributed music to it. But when we arrived at the theater, the R rating on the poster gave me pause. The many sermons with diatribes about how the entertainment industry was corrupting us with its diet of sex and violence came to mind. Apparently, this film had some of both, especially the latter, so I drew myself to my full righteous stature, and we didn't go in.

We did get good exposure to another one of the moral threats to society, rock music. I called my high school friend Alan, as I always did when visiting New Jersey, and he told me Mike Fennelly was in town. He also was in transit, on his way to England to record his first solo LP, *Lane Changer*. Crabby Appleton had broken up, and Mike had a solo contract with Epic, who had lined up one of our music heroes, Chris White of the Zombies, to produce.

Alan and Mike came to my house, Angie was there, so the four of us sat on the patio and Mike and I pulled out guitars. Mike looked the rock star, with hair and scarf both flowing. He played some of the songs he would record in England, and I played him some of my songs, one or two I had written with Andy, my roommate in Boston, and some of my own. He liked the latter better. I had a small Panasonic cassette recorder and taped our session.

I went into New York City a second time. Al Leiter, who had been my boss when I worked as a photo researcher for the *Plain Truth*, had suggested I visit some of our photo sources in the city. I visited Black Star, Woodfin Camp, and had lunch with people from the Associated Press, who invited me to the Rainbow Room. It was a warm summer day; I had been used to sartorial habits in California and dressed accordingly. The restaurant was strictly jacket and tie, so I had to don an ill-fitting spare kept on hand for yokels like me. One's education doesn't only take place in the classroom. After lunch, I went to Brooks Brothers and bought a button-down shirt with blue and pink stripes and a navy foulard tie. I also stopped at Brentano's and bought some books on European history and politics from the remainder table.

One weekend Ken Westby was in town for services. He had pastored the congregations in Washington and Baltimore for years and was one of the newly-named eight regional directors who oversaw other pastors and congregations. I liked the low-key style of how he conducted services and got to know him better in the afternoon. He had been invited to lunch at the home of an elder who invited Angie and me to come as well.

Being in New Jersey also meant I could serve as the best man at the wedding of two of that year's Ambassador graduates. Ken and Colleen had been a couple when they came into the church in New Jersey. They applied for college and went to separate campuses, Colleen to Big Sandy, Ken, to Bricket Wood. We didn't know each other well, all having attended different campuses, but Ken and I had something in common. He also had been in a school band with someone who had gone on to a professional career. In Ken's case, it was Bruce Springsteen.

After these activity-filled weeks, it was time to fly to Europe. Tante Mudel, my dad's younger sister—the one with whose family I had spent the summer in Europe nine years earlier—drove me to Kennedy Airport in her roomy white Oldsmobile. Mom and Tante Tilly, widow of one of my dad's brothers, rode with us. A button fell off the cuff of my new shirt, and Tante Tilly (I didn't know that ladies carried needle and thread with them) sewed it back on while I stuck my arm back from the front seat. We arrived, said our goodbyes, and I checked in for my Sabena flight.

After boarding and settling into my seat, a stewardess asked if I were traveling alone. Tourist class was full, and first-class nearly empty; I was invited to move there, one of only two times in my life that has happened to me. In those days, the upper deck of the 747 was a lounge so that first-class passengers could move around during the flight. I would have been too excited to sleep anyway, and the change meant I was more comfortable while watching the orange stripe at the horizon to our left.

When our flight landed at Brussels's Zaventem Airport, and we deplaned, I couldn't help notice the prominently-placed soldiers cradling automatic guns. Those were the days of airplane hijackings as a common form of terrorism; I don't know if security was stricter in Europe than in the States, but it was more visible. I went through immigration and customs, then waited for an hour for the money exchange office to open so that I could get a coin to call Ray Kosanke to let him know I'd arrived.

Ray picked me up, and we drove in his white Mercedes diesel straight to a press briefing at the headquarters of the Supreme Headquarters Allied Powers Europe (SHAPE) near Mons. After being awake all night, the first drowsiness set in as we flitted through the Belgian countryside. While the press spokesman droned on, my head nodded repeatedly, but not in agreement with what he was saying.

Mingling afterward with other journalists, I was sent up in the way the British like to send up Americans. Along with my blue blazer and the new striped shirt, I was wearing a rep tie. An English journalist recognized it as a regimental, named the outfit, and asked when I had served. A second wardrobe blunder in less than three weeks. I had not learned everything I would need to know at Ambassador.

Ray and I drove from there to the village where Ray lived with his wife Daniele with their daughters in a small bungalow, Plancenoit, close to the battlefield of Waterloo. I settled in for the night, but in mid-June, it is only dark for a short while, since Belgium lies further north than New Jersey or Southern California. One of the neighbors was taken with Donovan's newest single, "I Like You." A pleasant enough track, unless played repeatedly through the short, waking night. It took me a few days to begin sleeping through the night.

Until my arrival, Ray had been working from his home. We now set out to find two places, an apartment for me and an office for us to share. The instruction from Pasadena was to keep expenses for office rental low, and my salary dictated the same for my rent. I looked at apartments in my price range at the edge of the Brussels sprawl. Danièle, who was Belgian, helped me interpret the listings in *Le Soir*, the Brussels daily newspaper. When I called and inquired in my halting French, the landlords often said the apartment had already been rented, which made Danièle curious, so she called the most recent landlord who had turned me down. The landlord assured her that the apartment was still available and described it in glowing terms.

After a few days, Ray and I looked at an apartment in a seven-story apartment building in the Avenue de la Joyeuse Entrée, close to the Berlaymont, the starfish-shaped headquarters of the EC commission. There were two for rent, both owned by a man who had purchased and renovated them as an investment. One was on the sixth floor and one on the seventh, both with the same floor plan. The kitchen renovation on the sixth floor wasn't finished. The apartment on the seventh floor was furnished and ready to let, but the other interested us more since we could furnish it to meet our needs. Ray and I decided that if I lived in the apartment and paid half the rent, then both office and my living costs would be affordable. We moved into the ready apartment temporarily, then relocated downstairs when that apartment was ready.

The apartment had two rooms facing the street. The front half of the larger room became Ray's office. Somehow, we fit his large desk into the creaky elevator, then placed it in front of the street-facing windows. Ray located a used, inexpensive, but presentable seating arrangement for the other half of the room. The smaller room, just off the vestibule inside the front door, became my office. I bought an inexpensive trestle-desk in unfinished wood at Galeries Anspach; the telex machine we leased took its place in that room as well. With the nine-hour time difference between Brussels and Pasadena, most messages arrived in the middle of the night. The rattling sound of automatic typing and the ringing bell were loud enough to wake me, though I slept in the other end of the apartment.

Both front rooms looked out over the street, divided in the middle by an open section of the Belliard Tunnel, affording more than once a glimpse of Henry Kissinger's motorcade racing to the airport. Across the street lay the Parc Cinquantenaire, a large urban park created in 1880 to commemorate fifty years of Belgian independence.

The back half of the apartment served as my living area. There was a middle room, a bath (with bidet, something I hadn't seen before), and, all the way in the back, a bedroom. Both the bedroom and the kitchen overlooked a back alley.

Another necessary piece of business in those first days in Europe was to apply for credentials from the foreign correspondents' association as well as gaining accreditation at the European Community and NATO. Once that was arranged, Ray and I settled down to work. A fixed point on our schedule was the daily briefing in the press room of the Berlaymont. The chief spokesman was Italian, and it took me a while to begin to understand his heavily accented French.

I set about trying to make myself useful and productive. The *Plain Truth* was planned for the next ten months, through next May, and I didn't appear in the plan, but I began sending photographs, article ideas, research, and interviews. Ray was a cautious, sober man with an analytical mind. He read, listened, gathered information; I was more impulsive and temperamental. Also, I had been told in Pasadena that I was being sent over to "light a fire under Ray." Ray had written few articles, and the administration felt that there was little return on the costs of maintaining an office in an expensive world capital like Brussels. This reinforced my proclivity toward output as a way of measuring results. Not content with Ray's pace, I sent some articles to the new church newspaper, the *Worldwide News*, and also began a column in the *Portfolio*, where I could write more freely than what Ray considered appropriate for the *Plain Truth*. It was natural that Ray resented my impatience, so our first few months of working together were rocky.

My impediment was that I had much to learn. My French wasn't bad for an American, but using it as my daily working language was a challenge. Early in the summer, I bought my first issue of the *Economist*, the British newsweekly, and took it with me to read at the table while I supped in a cafe. I began to have a sense of how much I didn't know. My knowledge of European history and politics was probably higher than that of the average American, but that wasn't saying much. And although I had taken a basic, one-semester economics course in Boston, it became clear I barely grasped the rudiments. I set out on an ambitious reading program with an emphasis on economics and European history.

A particularly disturbing read was Albert Speer's insider account of Hitler's court. The charisma of the man at the center serving as the projection of the hopes of those around him, thus having his every whim, no matter how mad, enabled by the blind loyalty of his inner circle evoked memories of scenes I had witnessed in Pasadena. I suppressed this thought, but never rid myself of it entirely.

It wasn't long before I risked getting fired again. One of the tensions in Europe at the time, along with the long-simmering cold war, was the so-called cod war. It was a dispute over fishing rights between the nations that ringed the North Sea. The *Plain Truth* planned an article on it, to be reported by a writer coming over from Pasadena. I was to meet him in England, whence we would travel together to Iceland; I was to take photos.

I had purchased my plane ticket for the first leg of the trip, the flight to England, when a call from Pasadena informed me that the trip to Iceland was canceled.

What was I to do? The news had reached me with bags packed. I decided to take my flight to England anyway, even if it meant not being reimbursed for the cost of the ticket. I had been eager to make the trip. And if it meant being fired for disobeying an instruction, I felt I'd rather go down for attempting to do too much, instead of sitting around and doing too little. In addition to a possible contribution to the magazine, it would mean my first visit to the college's campus in Bricket Wood, near St. Albans in the Green Belt north of London.

The stay in Bricket Wood refreshed me. It was orientation weekend; the new school year was getting underway. I could sleep in one of the dorms. Paul, one of Charles Hunting's three children, was the room monitor, and it turned out my friend Randy was one of his best friends, so Paul and I hit it off well. The room had one more bunk than student. Paul told me I was welcome to stay there any time I came to visit.

Another of the seniors, Melvin, editor of the Bricket Wood iteration of the *Portfolio*, was from Grimsby, one of the fishing ports affected by the fishing rights dispute. He borrowed a car, and we drove to his home, providing my first taste of family life in the British working class. His father was a Marxist and only read the *Daily Worker*. Melvin's form of youthful rebellion was to be high Tory and read the *Telegraph*. Over a breakfast of pudding-and-pie, I listened to their passionate back-and-forth. That was after Melvin and I had gone to the docks at first light, and I photographed fishers unloading trawlers and setting up the fish market. The photos turned out well. I was disappointed that the article had been killed.

Also on campus at the time was Mike, fresh from the

Jerusalem Dig. He planned to observe the Feast of Tabernacles in England and spend the weeks until then there. We attended a few classes and went to London to visit the British Museum, then he decided to return with me to Brussels until the feast.

I enjoyed my stays in Bricket Wood that year. In a way, it was like an informal fourth year of Ambassador for me. I usually stayed in the dorm, but on one trip, the Plaches invited me to stay with them. Ruth deposited a tray with tea and biscuits outside my bedroom door when it was time to rise. She had adapted quickly to British ways of hospitality. When I came downstairs, I found Richard huddled with Charles Hunting in the living room. They immediately broke off their hushed conversation when I came in. Something was afoot. Subsequent events suggested to me what they may have been talking about. But I was not privy to it at the time.

Meanwhile, there was much going on in Europe and in the world. Just before I left for the feast in Minehead, David Price, director of the Bricket Wood News Bureau, came to Brussels with his wife, Sheila, for the Day of Atonement. That evening, we broke our fast at one of the city's best restaurants, Le Cygne. It was the first time I ate calf brains, apparently a delicacy; this was long before anyone had heard of mad cow disease. After dinner, David and Sheila came with Mike and me to see the office before returning to their hotel.

Something didn't seem right—I noticed soldiers with carbines at the ready posted on our street, but in my contented state after good food and wine, I didn't wonder about it. The next morning, I listened to the radio news on the American Armed Forces Network and learned that war had broken out in the Middle East. The presence of the soldiers became clear. The Iraqi embassy occupied the building next door, and there was a mosque in the corner of the Parc Cinquantenaire; its *iman* lived in the apartment across the hall from me. I had to smile at the lack of nose for news on the part of we three journalists the night before.

The continuing war, which was neither as one-sided nor as short as the one six years earlier, was an additional factor to our sobering celebration of the feast that year. One young woman attending was an American who lived on a Kibbutz near the Golan Heights. She had been observing Atonement there on her own, resting on a small balcony outside her room, and idly noticed fighter jets overhead. She thought it strange that the air force would do a training run on a high holy day, then it struck her that the jets were flying in the wrong direction—they were coming from Syria.

In those days, there were two choices for attending the church's Feast of Tabernacles in Europe. The French-speaking brethren, including the members of the Brussels congregation, went to Praz-sur-Arly, in the French Alps, and everyone else went to Minehead, a resort on the southern coast of the Bristol Channel, not far from Thomas Hardy country. We all stayed in a Butlin's holiday camp, an experience I'm glad I had so that I can understand references to it, but one which I had no desire to repeat. The weather was cold and rainy all week, with the clouds only parting shortly before sunset to gloriously usher in the Last Great Day, the eighth day of the feast. The only heat available in our small rooms (I shared one with a young Austrian who had just begun attending services) was a coin-operated space heater. The return of heat per coin struck me as meager. The weather was so miserable that Charles Hunting didn't take off his overcoat when he strode to the lectern for his sermons. Particularly for Hunting, this was not a joyous feast. His wife, morbidly suffering from cancer, remained home in Bricket Wood, and listened to services over a phone hook-up.

Nevertheless, there were many reasons for me to choose Minehead. I was English-speaking, so understanding the services would be much easier; I was still struggling to comprehend the messages in French at the bi-weekly service in Brussels. Also, the German churches went there, as did the Dutch, including my friend from my first semester in Pasadena, Jan. The Dutch even drafted me for their team in the international soccer tournament held that week. The Bricket Wood students would be there too, offering a bit of social life. I even added my voice to the tenor section of the Ambassador Chorale for special music.

And there was one more reason to go there. Margie, with whom I'd been involved in an on-again, off-again way in Pasadena, planned to transfer there, and I intended to tell her I was no longer afraid to commit. On a visit to London on my way, I had bought her a facsimile of the Folio edition of Shakespeare's plays as a gift. But she didn't come. Transfers had to be approved by the Festival Office, and she was told the site was full. There had been three applications for each available space. If she wanted to transfer somewhere, there were still available places in Alaska. So, she went, as did a colleague of hers from Imperial School, and a romance blossomed, as I learned when she next wrote. Coping with her absence, I had to rejoice with others. Nancy, a classmate, had come over to Minehead to be present when her best friend, on whom I had had a crush in Pasadena, announced her engagement. Now, one morning before services, Nancy came to me flushed and joyful. She was to be married, as well.

In Europe, we were at one remove from the continuing instability at headquarters, but not completely isolated. Al Carrozzo attended in Minehead with his family; this meant he could spend time with his mentor, Rod Meredith. Some of the sermons, particularly from Richard Plache, focused on the need to repair relationships, so I thought of my low opinion of Carrozzo. To me, he seemed an example of the Peter Principle—someone promoted above his level of competence. No doubt, I judged him too harshly. He had sold a successful business to become more involved in the church, and while Meredith's patronage accounted in part for his swift rise, I'm sure he was serious in his conviction to live a Christian life. My attitude toward him had worsened when, midway through the spring semester of our senior year, he was catapulted into Epistles of Paul class.

Now I felt the need to repent of my bad attitude toward him, confess and ask his forgiveness. I walked over to where he was sitting after one of the services, sat next to him and apologized, saying that I thought his assignment to teach Epistles was merely political.

He couldn't mask the bitterness of his response. "Of course, it was political," he replied, "it was all political." At the time, I didn't connect the dots. When Ted Armstrong was banished, Carrozzo, as one of Rod Meredith's two deputies in Church Administration, would have handled many of the questions of field ministers. Which rumors had he confirmed in his own disgust over Ted Armstrong's behavior, which confidences had he shared?

Carrozzo resigned from Worldwide shortly after returning home to California. I don't know if he had come to England to allow Meredith to try to talk him out of this step, perhaps even to urge Meredith to leave with him, or if it was to say goodbye.

I spent another two weeks in Bricket Wood after the feast. Dibar Apartian, director of the French-speaking

216

work, was there, on his way home from Praz-sur-Arly. His first question when he saw me: "Where were you?" Even though I attended services in Brussels, it never occurred to me that he would assume that I would consider the French feast site my assignment. Since English was my mother-tongue, I had assumed otherwise.

I finally returned to Brussels in early November, after a month in England. Gene and Barbara Hogberg, who had been in France for the feast, arrived in Brussels the next day. They visited the office and suggested I join them for a bite. I pulled on my only winter coat, a short suede jacket with fake fur collar I had bought at J.C. Penney in Pasadena. Definitely not business attire. Barbara asked whether the church had given me a clothing allowance before I left for Europe. When she found out it hadn't, she and Gene took me to a men's store and bought a double-breasted navy overcoat out of money left over from their feast allotment (money given to church employees sent to travel to feast sites).

Ray had been in the States for the Feast and returned a couple of days after the Hogbergs passed through. A detente in the tense relation with Ray had come during Mike's stay with me before the Feast. Mike got on well to both Ray and me, and was, in addition to being a trained journalist, more athletic than I. He had played against Ray on the basketball courts in Pasadena. Mike led me out on a search through Brussels until we found a store that had an

American football, and the three of us passed it around the Cinquantenaire Park in the late autumn sunshine.

After Mike left, the fog rolled in. That first winter in Brussels seemed to be covered by an unbroken layer that rolled across Flanders in mid-November and didn't move until spring.

The work-week was interesting and fulfilling, but the weekends lonely. That was when I acutely felt the transition from college life, with weekend dates, meals in the student center, fellowship before and after services, and activities on Sunday. Ray went home on Friday evening to his family. Sometimes he took me along for supper; otherwise, I dined alone in my apartment. On the weekends I stayed in Brussels, the bi-weekly services—usually conducted by Jean Carion, a successful businessman who cared for the members in time he volunteered—meant getting out of the apartment to our rented meeting hall in the national library, near the royal palace. There was no one my age in the congregation, certainly no one to date. On some of the other weekends, I went to Holland to visit the family of my friend Jan. At the time, the services in Utrecht were in English. Almost all of the brethren spoke English as a second language, so it was easier to communicate with them than it was with the members of the Brussels congregation, although my French was slowly improving.

One person who would have welcomed some social contact was the stewardess who bumped me to first class on my flight over. She had contacted me soon after I settled into the office-apartment and invited me to attend a concert with her. During the flight, I had told her that I had sung in our college choir, and she suggested I audition for the choir she sang in, which specialized in Bach cantatas. Ray warned me off. From his days as a basketball player, he knew that lonely stewardesses used complementary upgrades as a way of meeting men. Since she was not "in the church," nothing good could come of it, he felt. I don't know whether I would have passed the audition, but I regret not having tried out. Baroque music, especially Bach, was experiencing a revival, especially in the Low Countries. Gustav Leonhardt and Nikolaus Harnoncourt had just begun their joint project of recording all the Bach Cantatas two years earlier.

Adding to the bleak autumnal mood was the oil embargo OPEC had introduced in the aftermath of the Yom Kippur War. Europe was more dependent on imported oil than the U.S., and once the novelty of empty autobahns filled with cyclists on auto-free Sundays wore off, the economic jolt and accompanying inflation created a sense of crisis. The ambitious timetable for further integration the European Community had adopted one year earlier on the eve of British entry was wordlessly shelved. Now the challenge was to maintain the solidarity that had been achieved so far in the face of economic contraction. The more optimistic of European leaders suggested that it was precisely in a time of crisis that developments became possible that otherwise wouldn't happen, but it sounded like brave whistling on a cold wintry night.

The year drew to a close. The affairs of the EC wound down as people took a Christmas and New Year's break. I took advantage of the slower pace to drive with Jan and his brother Paul to Paris to visit another classmate, Bob, a ministerial trainee there. In our time together, it became clear that he was going through many of the same experiences as I; in fact, he seemed to be having an even harder time of it. The pastor charged with his training repeatedly made him feel that he was a foolish, uncultured, immature American.

My sympathy for Bob made me realize that my situation was not as bad. Still, the year 1973 ended with me in an introspective mood. In my self-assessment, I was youthful, unruly, and boastful. My outbursts of ill-timed exuberance were even more out-of-place in Europe than they would have been at home in America. I remained eager to contribute vibrant articles about world-shaking events, but my ambition outstripped both opportunity and ability.

The traditional Christmas break in Europe ends with Epiphany, January 6. After that, the normal business of the EC would resume. That day fell on a Sunday in 1974, and I used it for a fast. For the umpteenth time, I devoted it to the question of discerning the will of God in the matter of marriage. Now that the question of how I would serve the

Work seemed sorted out—however tenuously—I finally felt ready to commit, but to whom? Since Margie had another interest, I corresponded with three—Angie, the Big Sandy coed I had dated while stopping at home on my way to Brussels, as well as two Bricket Wood coeds. In the latter two cases, they had initiated the correspondence. Was one of these three the right one, or someone else? I often woke from a terrifying dream. I was standing at the altar next to a veiled bride and was filled with panic that I didn't know who it was, but that now we were bound to each other.

I tried to approach the question in a spiritual way, of not seeking selfishly the one I wanted. But what would be the alternative: marrying the one who seemed to need me the most? I recoiled from the presumption behind that thought. How could I practice the way of "give"—as Herbert Armstrong paraphrased the law of love—in deciding whom to marry?

As the fast drew to a close, the insight struck me that, above all, it was God who practiced the way of giving. Rather than trying to decide between who would give me the most or to whom I could give the most, I should leave it in God's hands and let him be the giver. In the meantime, I should continue to work on myself so that I could be his gift to someone while trusting he was preparing someone to be a gift to me.

The next day brought some welcome social contact. Forty-five Bricket Wood students and two faculty members were taking advantage of the winter break to tour Europe. For many, it was their first visit to the continent. Brussels was their first stop after leaving the campus at quarter past five and crossing the Channel. I took advantage of a free seat on their bus to go with them for a somber visit to a cemetery at Ypres, "in Flanders fields." Five separate engagements had been fought there during the First World War, taking the lives of hundreds of thousands of combatants. Looking over rows and rows of white crosses drove home the horror and futility of war.

We returned to Brussels, and they checked into their hotel, the Duc de Brabant. After dinner, I showed them some of the sights of Brussels by night and accompanied them the next day on a tour of the Berlaymont, where the students had a chance, after a film and lecture, to engage in a question-and-answer session with an EC spokesman. That evening, I took one of them, Jann, to a movie at the American Library. I had to ask one of the faculty chaperones for permission, which he grudgingly gave.

The students left the following day, but I had more social contact to look forward to. I planned to go to Dusseldorf for the weekend, where a few more Bricket Wood students were spending the break helping in the office. But just before I left, there was a change of plans. There was a social planned in the Zurich congregation after services that week. The office choir (an octet) was to contribute entertainment, as well as sing in services. But one of the two tenors was sick—would I consider changing my plans? So, the following day, after taking the train from Brussels to Dusseldorf, I boarded the office's Volkswagen van—similar to the one in which I had first toured Europe a decade earlier—bound for Switzerland.

Six months earlier, I had flown to Brussels with two suitcases and a carry-on. The rest of what I had in Pasadena came in the container carrying Frank Schnee's household, together with an American car he had purchased. A few weeks after I arrived in Brussels, Ray received word that the container had arrived in Dusseldorf, so we drove there to pick up my belongings. As we stood and talked with Schnee in the family room, a young woman traipsed in. She was one of a group of young people playing volleyball in the backyard, a young German woman working in the office that summer between her third and fourth years at Bricket Wood.

My guard went up.

I had been warned before leaving Pasadena that both Mr. and Mrs. Schnee had a reputation of matchmakers. The Dusseldorf *Büro* was irreverently called the marriage bureau. The thought went through my mind, "so this is who they have me matched up with; we'll see about that." As it turned out, it had been a misunderstanding. One of the young people spotted us through the window and said to the others, "Ray Kosanke is here, and Henry Sturcke is with him." The young woman in question misheard my name as that of a recent Bricket Wood graduate, Stirk. Over the years, I've had ample experience of her misunderstanding what she heard. But I didn't know that at the time.

Ray and I stayed overnight and visited the office the next day. Among the stops we made was the Editorial Department, where this young woman was at her desk, working on a revised edition of the *Wonderful World Tomorrow* book. In my short time working in Editorial in Pasadena, the booklet art director, with whom I shared an office, had passed that project to me so that I could try my hand at layout design. I hadn't heard anything more about that after I was fired. Now I was pleasantly surprised to see that my ideas had survived.

Interestingly, I had met her parents two weeks before that. They were part of the small congregation in Hamburg, two of its more outgoing members. They welcomed me and reminded me of my own aunts and uncles.

I had traveled to Hamburg in northern Germany on a Friday, shared a room with one of the Dusseldorf office workers that night, and attended services the next morning in a hotel on the Alster. Schnee asked me to lead songs, I didn't think to ask him the best way to ask the congregants to rise for the hymns. My resultant command "*Stehen Sie auf!*" would have struck the members as rude if it hadn't sounded so comical coming from this young man struggling to speak German in public. The Ambassador students on the Bad Oeynhausen language program were visiting the Hamburg congregation that day, so after services, I spent part of the afternoon with them at *Planten un Blomen*, which I had visited for the first time nine years earlier. The I took a train to Bremervörde, where my aunt, Tante Mudel, picked me up at the station. She and Uncle George were visiting our relatives there again that summer. But there was another uncle in Germany, unplanned. Uncle Herman, my dad's oldest brother, had been in Africa with his wife. He had been suffering from cancer and had now taken a turn for the worse. I drove with Tante Mudel and Uncle George to the hospital in Bremerhaven. It seemed disjointed to go to the *Schützenfest*, the annual marksman's festival, that evening. My cousins Evelyn and Carl, Herman's children, were there as well. They had flown over to take leave of their father.

A week or two after picking up my belongings, I returned to Dusseldorf for the wedding of one of the ministerial trainees, a graduate of Bricket Wood. I was still adjusting to relying on public transportation. In the U.S., using automobiles, if you left five minutes late, you could easily make it up on the road. Now, leaving the house a few minutes late made it likely I would miss the subway connection that would take me to the main station for my train to Cologne, where I would switch to another for Dusseldorf. I was used to subways from New York and Boston. No worries, the next one comes along in a few minutes. Here, the waits between were a little longer, and the train to Cologne had pulled out by the time I got to the *Gare Centrale* and reached the platform. The next one would be in two hours. I made the trip anyway, but by the time I reached the Schnee's home, the ceremony was long over, and all had gone to the reception; I didn't know where that was. I knocked at doors until I found one person who hadn't gone to the reception and could tell me where to go. I arrived; the meal had been served. But then the same young woman who had traipsed in from volleyball two weeks earlier came to meet me at the entrance to the room, led me to a free seat at one of the tables, and made sure I received something to eat. I was grateful to her and danced with her that evening more than with any other.

Just like the misunderstanding of my name, I didn't know at the time that she had been assigned to keep a lookout for late arriving guests and make sure they were accommodated.

At the feast in Minehead, I dated nearly every day. One coed whom I did not date was the young German woman whom I thought the Schnees wanted to match me with. I enjoyed her solo performance of "Shall We Dance," which she sang during the entertainment evening, as her brother Wolfgang waltzed her around the stage. I even had lunch one day with her parents. Another day, I spotted her with her parents walking a hundred yards or so ahead of me. She spontaneously threw her arm around her mother's waist, and the thought occurred to me, so strongly that it almost seemed a voice in my head, "Of all the girls that you've known, that one would make the best wife and mother." I wasn't in love with her, it was simply an observation. And I have no doubt that many of the other girls I'd loved have been wonderful wives and mothers. Implicit in this insight were the words, "for you."

Later, I found that she was so furious with me as she watched me date her classmates that she hoped I would finally ask her out so that she could turn me down.

Now, this girl, Edel, who had come from Bricket Wood to Dusseldorf for the winter break, was one of the eight in the office choir.

We were all quartered in the homes of members. Four of us stayed on a farm in Stetten. I shared one room with the other tenor, two of the women in the choir shared another room. After settling in, we drove to Zurich in the office's Volkswagen van and arrived in time for services at the Baur au Lac, where the social also took place. That evening, I danced only with the woman who misheard my name, who was staying on the same farm (I didn't know that Esther Schnee had asked her to help arrange the housing assignments). Driving back out of Zurich along the old highway 1 as it made its ascent toward Bremgarten, the lights of the city and the stars over the mountains seemed to have additional sparkle.

At the farmhouse, we sat around for a while, although

it was late. The two of us sat on the ledge of a *Kachelofen*, a tiled wood stove, and warmed our hands with sacks of cherry pits. The warm feeling grew, but maybe it wasn't just from the stove. The others were impatient to get to bed, but we were in no hurry to break off our conversation. As Dylan once sang, "Why wait any longer for the one you love when she's standing in front of you?"

The next day we all drove back to Dusseldorf, taking a break to romp in the snow, then I continued on to Brussels. Now I knew who I would marry.

Long-distance courtship was an interesting experience. Edel went back to Bricket Wood for her final semester, I settled down to work in Brussels. We wrote and telephoned. At the end of February, I traveled to England for a week—my third visit to Bricket Wood since arriving in Europe. I timed this visit to coincide with a crucial British election. I went to London on election day, visiting the editorial offices of the *Economist* in the afternoon, then spent the evening with David Price as the returns came in. It was a winter of discontent in that dark, strike-ridden country. Edward Heath, who had led the belated entry of Great Britain into the European Community the previous year (contrary to Herbert Armstrong's predictions based on little other than the presumption that the British were descended from the Israelite tribe of Ephraim), now faced turmoil. He called an early election, the first general election after the U.K. entered the EC; it came in the doldrums of an oil-starved winter.

The general feeling of the country was reflected in the result, which slowly came in as David took me around to the election headquarters of the Conservatives, Labour, and the Liberals. We wandered from Conservative Party Central Office to Transport House (both on Smith Square) to the Savoy Hotel, where Conservative supporters had hoped to celebrate in a swank setting. Harold Wilson seemed tired and didn't speak well. Edward Heath seemed very stiff. By contrast, Jeremy Thorpe, the Liberal leader, spoke well, displayed good wit and evidence of a sharp mind. When we checked back at the Savoy at three in the morning, the ballroom was deserted, except for the waiters picking up the tablecloths.

Although the Conservatives retained a narrow lead in votes cast, it became clear they would fall short of a parliamentary majority and were in no mood to celebrate. They not only lost seats to Harold Wilson's Labour Party but also to a resurgent Liberal Party, which nearly tripled its share of the popular vote, its best showing in more than half-a-century. Under the first-past-the-post system, however, this resulted in only thirteen seats and a long list of valiant seconds. Nevertheless, it appeared by the end of a long night that ended with no clear victor that they might hold the balance of power. We finished with an early breakfast at the Cavendish near Piccadilly.

Contrasted to the bleak news was the budding romance. My trip to England coincided with a dance put on by the sophomores, to which I took Edel, but was otherwise discrete. I made sure to date others for Bible study and Sabbath services. I knew that if everyone knew she was taken, then she would have little social life that semester. Two of the Carions' three children attended Bricket Wood. One of them, Michelle, roomed with Edel, which helped to communicate in a non-obvious way. The other, Olivier, became a good friend.

A sense of crisis continued throughout early 1974, not only in the U.K. but throughout Europe. Council of Ministers' meetings often went through the night, unable to reach the required unanimous decision on proposals submitted by the commission. Jack Benny, the comedian whose age remained thirty-nine for decades, would have approved as the clock stayed at one minute to midnight for hours while I waited in the hallway with other journalists.

Occasionally one of the participants would come out and give us tidbits. The most entertaining of them was Christopher Soames, one of the two British commissioners, whose manner at times recalled that of his father-in-law, Winston Churchill.

Henry Kissinger's peripatetic travels regularly brought him through Brussels as well. An old joke alleged that whenever he boarded his plane, and the pilot asked, "Where to?" he would answer, "it doesn't matter, we have problems everywhere." This didn't seem to be his attitude, though. He relished his role. Even initiatives he had a hand in on the other side of the world became palpable where we were, as the reception I attended when the Chinese news agency opened an office in Brussels demonstrated. Beginning with Klaus Mehnert's visit to Pasadena, I had read several books on China, so I was eager to question one of their journalists closely about his experiences as a student during the cultural revolution. Both he and the country seemed to be recovering from it.

The more essential Kissinger seemed for resolution of the oil crisis, the more concern Europeans felt over a weakened Nixon. There was little understanding of the drawn-out Watergate procedure, especially in the wake of Willy Brandt's sudden and dramatic resignation. Even before that April morning, when I had awoken early and heard that surprising news from Bonn on the radio, Europeans had been asking me why Nixon didn't just resign so that the U.S. could get on with exercising its role in the world.

Chapter Twelve

The winter of discontent on the world scene was mirrored by events in Worldwide. A half-year earlier, when I left Pasadena, Ted Armstrong had been consolidating executive control. In July, as I was settling in Brussels, Herbert Armstrong named him his successor. This didn't stop unsettling rumors from the U. S. reaching us.

It seemed to be the delayed effect of 1972, both the disappointment over the non-begin of the great tribulation and the lingering effects of Ted Armstrong's moral problems. There was growing pressure for doctrinal change, not in central tenets of the church, but in matters that had an impact on the lives of members: healing, tithing, and the church's stance on divorce and remarriage. Another issue was the long-simmering question of the correct day to observe Pentecost, which the church kept on Monday.

Many hoped that Ted Armstrong could use his influence to help his father accept changes; these hopes were quickly frustrated. Others resisted any change. Prominent among these were men who had been students in the earliest years of the college. The first students were, in a sense, surrogate sons for Herbert Armstrong, unlike Ted Armstrong, who, in an act of rebellion, joined the navy during the Korean War, becoming a disappointment to his father and heartache for his mother.

Ted Armstrong was caught in a double-bind. Some accused him of introducing liberalism into the church; others became disenchanted with him when things didn't change fast enough. Nor did it help that he had overextended himself in his desire to control every aspect of the church in addition to his grueling writing and broadcasting schedule. As a manager, he seemed to be flailing.

Opposition to doctrinal adjustment often went hand-in-hand with continued concern over the moral failings that had come to light two years earlier, although it also served as an issue for the would-be reformers when matters came to a head as the year closed. For them, the lengths to which Herbert Armstrong had been willing to go to cover up his son's transgressions seemed to parallel his stubborn resistance to an open discussion of doctrinal questions.

In December, a pastor in Shreveport, La., announced his resignation, and the reasons for it, from the pulpit, splitting the congregation. Soon after that, three regional pastors resigned, including George Kemnitz, whom I had admired as a teacher in Pasadena, and Ken Westby, whom I had met just before flying overseas, as well as many of the pastors in their regions. Apparently, they had been discussing how to effect reforms in the church, but the Shreveport pastor jumped the gun and forced their hand.

My mentor, John, was back in the field, pastoring a church. We corresponded, but his letters contained ominous advice. Finally, a letter from him arrived to tell me he had resigned. The letter had been preceded by a premonition that I needed to write to him first. In my letter to him, I rehearsed that we had first met when he came to my dorm room in Boston as a representative of Herbert Armstrong and the Worldwide Church of God.

When his letter arrived, I phoned Charles Hunting in Bricket Wood, who was able to calm me. In the course of our conversation, though, he mentioned without going into details that my mentor had been an object of mercy from his student days on. I was left to wonder what that might have meant.

When the dust settled, the church had lost thirty or so ministers, including a significant portion of pastors of congregations. But few followed them. Average weekly attendance in the U.S. dropped by about two thousand; some of those who dropped out stopped attending anywhere. For all the frustration and disappointment, few switched their allegiance. Many perhaps felt, as I did, that we had only met these ministers because they represented

Herbert Armstrong. Meanwhile, a backlog of visit requests from people interested in the church had piled up, so the loss wasn't felt for long once many of them were invited to services.

Ernest Martin, who had long seen the error in our calculation of when to observe Pentecost, resigned and started a foundation for biblical research. At first, his marketing efforts were to church members, with his literature focused on issues that had stirred controversy, such as tithing and details of prophetic interpretation. Other than that, his basic teachings resembled those of Worldwide. Later, he gained a bit of renown in wider circles with books claiming he could identify the star of Bethlehem with astronomical phenomena, or establish the correct order of the canon of the Bible. These, too, were topics he had taught in his Worldwide years. He also developed his own theory of the location of Solomon's Temple, just south of what is commonly accepted to be the Temple Mount.

The lack of success of the new association formed by the pastors who left revealed one of Herbert Armstrong's strengths: he was an entrepreneur with a dominant personality. I was not the only one who believed that any contribution I could make to bringing a message of hope to the world was magnified by my support of his efforts. Still, a number of those who remained, while convinced that Worldwide was "the true church," believed it could be much better than it was.

Herbert Armstrong's response to the explosion was at first high-handed and deceitful. Rather than dealing with the issues raised, he emphasized his and Ted Armstrong's special calling. Anyone who harbored suspicions was rebelling against God. As tempers cooled, however, he followed the recommendations of a newly-formed doctrinal committee and approved changes in all of the issues that had been questioned.

My soundtrack in those bleak winter days was Dylan's first release after leaving Columbia for Arista, *Planet Waves*. His output since the misguided *Self Portrait*, which came out shortly before I left for Pasadena, had been meager. *New Morning* had been good, but not essential in the way the series of LPs that culminated in *Blonde on Blonde* had been. It had seemed a reaction to the tumult of the 1960s, a retreat to domesticity that mirrored my refuge at Ambassador.

I bought a cassette of the new release and played it in the portable Panasonic recorder I had bought in the college's commissary before leaving Pasadena. The new morning of domestic bliss had dissipated. Not completely: there were two or three songs of devoted, committed love, as well, but it was symptomatic that two songs, "Wedding Song" and "Dirge," seemed so interchangeable that I sometimes forgot they were two separate songs. The prevailing mood was set by songs of urgent desire and unsatisfactory relationships.

The standout tracks, to me, were two other songs. One of these, "Never Say Goodbye," evoked deep Minnesota winter and a nostalgically-tinged yearning to hold on to a relationship that might be in the deep-freeze as well. Whereas the album had opened, on a night like this—cabin-snug in front of a roaring fire—now the persona of the singer and his companion, whether they were indoors or out, were fully aware of the sub-zero temperatures. Generous space afforded Robbie Robertson's guitar lines between the verses simulated a dialogue. There was no refrain, no middle-eight, just five stanzas of four lines each—more fragment than finished song—yet it haunted me, and I played it repeatedly. The other exception, "Forever Young," unfolded more slowly. It too seemed unfinished, although the lyrics, a rich intonation of blessings, were fine. Yet it seemed as if Dylan and the Band hadn't reached common ground on how to play it and included two attempts, one to close the first side and the other to open the second. Each version had its strengths, but neither seemed to do the song justice.

Gradually, almost imperceptibly, the days grew longer. As my first winter in Europe, where the nights were longer than what I had experienced in the States, drew to a close, the air softened, and occasionally we had perfect spring days of sunshine. Ray and I began to develop a comfortable working relationship. One factor in the improvement was unintentional. On one of his trips, either to Pasadena or to cover a conference in another city, I typed a daily news summary in an aerogram and mailed it to him. He saw in that the seeds of a way we could contribute what we were covering in a form that might be useful for the news bureau or the telecast. Ted Armstrong began having Ray do telephone reports as well, coaching him in presentation, and using some of the reports in the radio program.

One of the most interesting stories I covered, though, was one that turned out to be a non-story—fake news, as it would be called today. Ray returned from a trip to Pasadena with a news clipping handed to him by a secretary in the publishing department who asked why we didn't know about this. The article described a powerful mainframe computer in the headquarters of the EC, the Berlaymont, one block away from us. Two stories high, it was used to generate a six-digit identity code for each citizen of the member nations.

The fear this instilled was more than a Luddite resistance to digitalization. The thirteenth chapter of Revelation, a key text for all prophecy buffs, with its vision of the two beasts—a ten-horned civil power that rises from the sea and a beast that rises from the land and combines the features of a lamb and a dragon—closes with the prediction that all would have to receive a mark on their hand or forehead, and that anyone not having that mark would be excluded from economic life. In a final flourish, the ancient practice of gematria (hiding and revealing names by use of the equivalent numerical value of letters of the alphabet) is invoked, and the number of the beast is given as 666 (Rev. 13: 16–18).

The article named the head of the department responsible for it and mentioned that some of those working on the project lovingly called the machine "the Beast." The story had appeared in *Moody Monthly*, a fundamentalist Christian magazine, and was presented as the fulfillment of the "mark of the Beast" from the book of Revelation.

Ray dropped the clipping on my desk and said that this was a good reporting opportunity for me. It was too late for the *Plain Truth* to break the story—we had been scooped, but we certainly should report it. So, I went to work on it. The list of contacts I had developed since arriving in Brussels was still short but included a British national who worked as a programmer for the EC. I invited him to a drink to learn more about his work. Nothing about personal identity, it had more to do with road use and traffic patterns for transportation planning. I asked him about his work station. There was no computer in Brussels. For his work, and the work of other departments, the EC leased time on a mainframe in Luxembourg.

Just in case it were a cover-up, I walked every floor of the Berlaymont. There was no sign of a two-story computer. I looked for the name mentioned in *Moody Monthly*, the directory turned up nothing, not even anything similar. Nor did a look at the nameplates outside the offices as I strolled the halls yield anything.

I wasn't disappointed that my work had turned up nothing. Not in the sense of no result, but a negative result: There was simply no story.

The incident helped me reflect on our mission. Ray and I were in Brussels, the headquarters of what we believed, along with the rest of the church, was the center of the coming United States of Europe. This final resurrection of the Holy Roman Empire would fulfill the prophecies of Daniel and Revelation and would signal the end of the age and precede the return of Jesus Christ. We were there to provide an eye-witness account of this.

What we found was a bureaucracy increasingly moribund as it wrestled with trade agreements and agricultural subsidies. To report as if something were happening when, in fact, it was not, ran counter not only to my training as a journalist but also to my deepest sense of right and wrong. If we were just going to spin tales, we could do that more cost-efficiently from a desk in the News Bureau in Pasadena. The only value we could offer Worldwide as a return on its investment was honest reporting on what was happening, and on what was not.

The reality that Europe was slowly losing track of the original impulses that had led to its formation was poignantly brought home on an evening honoring Ted Heath.

Prominently seated in the front row of the balcony was Jean Monnet. Monnet's inspiration for the European

Community came from his younger years as a sales representative in the U.S. for his family's cognac firm. The single currency and lack of borders he found there not only made business much simpler (and more profitable) than in Europe, but it also encouraged free movement of people and ideas. He dreamed of the day when Europe could achieve something similar. His vision fused with that of fellow Frenchman Robert Schuman, who, at the close of the Second World War and its destruction, felt that the time was ripe for integrating Germany into a larger framework that would redirect its energies away from expansion through military means.

It seemed ironic that the sense that the European project was stalling had come so quickly after Britain, Denmark, and Norway joined just a few months before I arrived in Europe. The hope at the time among more democratically-minded continentals was that the addition of these three nations with a strong democratic tradition would counteract the tendency toward unnecessary centralization and bureaucracy.

There had been three solid achievements of the European Community so far: the European Coal and Steel Community with which it had begun, the common market, which allowed free trade between the member states, and the common agricultural policy, although unlike the other two, it was not an unmixed success. Other policy initiatives were works in progress: a regional policy, a social policy (the ramification of the free movement of labor), energy policy, and a monetary union. Even farther off lay the prospects of united foreign or defense policies.

The improved working relation with Ray was also due to ways that the *Plain Truth* was changing that allowed more of an outlet for our contributions. Ted Armstrong had ended the daily telecast, frustrated with the twelve-week lead time each episode needed. A radio program had a quicker turnaround, allowing it to be timelier and more topical. Now, in line with this, he looked for ways to achieve the same with the magazine. Typically, an issue contained five to seven lengthy articles, planned many months in advance, and slanted to have timeless, universal appeal. Ted Armstrong's congenital impatience with this approach was abetted by his apocalyptic mind-set. He felt events in the Middle East had brought the world to the brink of Armageddon. While our date-setting may have been off, it didn't mean that the return of Jesus Christ had receded into the distant future. If our mission was to warn the world, then we had no time to waste.

His search for a way to make the magazine timelier came in two stages. To accommodate his sense of urgency, one signature of the basic core magazine became black-and-white, which shortened the production time considerably. This gave me my opportunity to break into print. My byline made its debut in October, the first issue reflecting the change, on an article about Britain's intention to renegotiate the terms of its membership (yes, nearly a half-century ago, and a little over a year after entry). From then until I left Europe, it was a rare issue that didn't contain one or two articles from me. The few that didn't invariably had one from Ray. We shared research, tossed ideas back and forth, and read each other's articles before submitting them. A highlight of our partnership was covering a summit newly-elected French president Giscard d'Estaing convoked in Paris in December 1974, just before France's six-month term presiding the council of ministers expired.

Representatives of each member nation held separate press briefings, intended for the press of their own nations. We Americans protested, and Leo Tindemans, Belgian prime minister, held a briefing for us. As I recall, in addition to Ray and me, the only other present was Dick Longworth from the Associated Press. At the final press conference, open to all, I garnered a front-row seat and took a photo of Giscard d'Estaing that ran at least three times in the church's publications.

The next time Edel and I saw each other after the week I spent in England at the end of February was for the spring holy days. She and her brother flew to Dusseldorf. I traveled there by train and met them. We went to dinner with them and their parents, then we drove together the next day to Eltville, in the wine region along the Rhine. Frank Schnee drafted me as one of the helpers to distribute bread and wine for our celebration of the Lord's

Supper, the first time I'd been tapped for that role. The next evening, we had a group meal, the Night to Be Much Observed (the time of the Jewish Passover observance; we stubbornly insisted they were wrong and that the Passover should be on the previous evening, based on our harmonization of the discrepancies in the Gospel accounts of the crucifixion). The next day, the first day of Unleavened Bread, was marked with two services. We had lunch with Edel's parents, then we took a walk along the Rhine before the afternoon service. I walked ahead with Edel's father, Edel dropped behind with her mother.

I was sensitive about being an American in Europe, and I wanted to be sure to do everything correctly, so I asked her father for her hand, without ever having mentioned the word marriage to her. He gave me some fatherly advice, then said he had only one condition: that I not take her away from Europe. Edel's mother had grown up in Lithuania and had come west to work during the war. When the war ended, her parents fled ahead of the Soviets and stopped in Thuringia, slated to be in the American occupation zone. At the last moment, the Americans traded it to the Soviets for Bavaria, so Edel grew up with one set of grandparents stranded in communist East Germany. Her mother suffered from seeing them so rarely, so Edel's father understandably didn't want her to suffer similar sorrow. At the time, I had no expectation of returning to the U.S., so I agreed. As we neared the hall, Edel and her mother caught up with us. Her father said this was wonderful news and that we would celebrate that night at dinner. Edel said it was too soon to celebrate, she wasn't sure. He replied that was fine, but we would celebrate anyway. I learned over the years that this was her usual response to big developments; evidently, he knew this. At any rate, I assured her she could take all the time she needed. At dinner that night, she slipped her hand into mine under the table, so I knew she had.

I treated myself to a seat in the first-class compartment on the train back to Brussels. The first leg of the trip was on the Lorelei Express along the Rhine. In those days, the difference between the two classes was noticeable, and I was in a mood to celebrate. Edel returned to Bricket Wood but soon passed through Brussels as part of the senior trip, a tour of Europe. I asked the faculty chaperone if I could tag along with the students that evening; with an air of reluctance, he approved. After dinner, as the group of us walked back to the students' hotel, I walked side-by-side with Edel, and the rest soon caught on, although we hadn't said anything. The next day, she got permission to visit the office.

I continued to spend most of my time alone but was no longer lonely. It was spring, and I was in love. On Sundays, I read, wrote letters, played my guitar, and sometimes went out exploring the city with my camera. Once I came across some Basque dancers. Another time there was a flea market in front of the main cathedral. I picked up a few household items, among them a used Philips electric coffee grinder, in Sixties-style pastel blue, and paid the equivalent of one dollar for it. It is still going strong more than forty-five years later.

I returned to Bricket Wood for graduation. At the grad ball, Richard Plache announced our engagement. Herbert Armstrong had flown from Pasadena. As a treat, he had included one of his secretaries in his traveling party in the church's Gulfstream II. This was the one who had given me a tender kiss on the cheek when we said goodbye a year earlier in Pasadena and said she would come to see me in Europe. I had not heard from her since, and now there was nothing left for us to do but for her to introduce me to Herbert Armstrong and for me to introduce her to Edel.

It was at least the fourth time I had been introduced to Herbert Armstrong, but since I was far off his radar, each time was like the first time to him.

We didn't know it at the time, but the graduation ceremony the next day was to be the last held at Bricket Wood, making Edel and her brother nearly the last to graduate there. Only the Wheatcroft siblings came after them in alphabetical order. We learned the news of the closing while Edel was visiting Belgium a few weeks after her graduation. We were enjoying a meal in the Carion home, their son Olivier was there as well. A phone call informed him that he would have to transfer to Pasadena to complete his studies (his sister Michelle was spending the summer with the Apartians in Pasadena, so heard the news more directly).

From Bricket Wood, I traveled with Edel to visit her family for a few days in Niebüll; I was looking forward to seeing her homeland. We took the ferry from Ipswich to Hook of Holland, then continued by train, our first extended trip as an engaged couple. I was careful, though, to observe the proprieties of Worldwide.

In northern Schleswig-Holstein, I found the farms and the people not so different from those in Lintig, the ancestral home on my father's side of the family, so I felt at home. The main difference was the landscape, with high dikes protecting the land from the North Sea. Edel took me to meet her paternal grandmother. Edel was her first granddaughter, but so many of her cousins had married that her Oma feared Edel would become an old maid.

Then she heard that Edel was to marry after all, but to an American, and that was worse. It brought back memories of the aftermath of the war, when many young women left as brides of (black) American G.I.s. When I walked in and greeted her in *Plattdeutsch*, everything was all right.

I returned to Brussels, Edel, to Dusseldorf, where she resumed her job as a translation checker in the Editorial Department. They had a good system, adapted from that used by *Reader's Digest*. Worldwide felt that its mission was to preach the gospel to all the world. The need to translate into other languages brought with it the need to ensure we were speaking the same thing. A few years earlier, there had been a flap over something that had appeared in print in *Die reine Wahrheit*, as the German edition of the *Plain Truth* was called in those days (the name had recently been changed to *Klar und Wahr*, a major improvement). The flap had cost the editor at the time his job.

Now the church used professional translators, at least one of whom identified strongly with our message. Then the translation was checked twice in-house. The first checker compared it line for line with the English original for accuracy, then the second read the German text alone for style and readability. At the time, the *Plain Truth* was at the cutting edge of international magazine production. As a first step, it had adopted a standard layout in all languages, with just the black plate changed for each language edition. By the end of 1973, it began exploring ways to regionally tailor the content, since not all articles interested people in all markets. The introduction of a black-and-white center signature in the U.S. edition created the possibility that the international editions could use this for regional content.

I was able to visit Dusseldorf a couple of times that summer; our wedding was our fifth or sixth date in the year since we had met.

Getting married wasn't easy, though. I was an American living in Belgium, and Edel was German. We were to be married in Germany, but the bureaucracies and laws of the three countries were involved. Both Belgium and Germany had retained one of the features of the Napoleonic Code, which dictated that a legal marriage could only be conducted by a civil authority. Edel was registered in Dusseldorf, so that was where the civil ceremony had to take place.

As committed church members, though, we believed that since God alone had the authority to bind and loose a couple, only a ceremony performed by a minister counted. So, we wanted a church ceremony, too. This, of course, should take place near her parents' home, near the Danish border. Frank Schnee agreed to perform it. There were now other ministers who could conduct the services scheduled on that late August weekend. Her father booked a hall for that date, and we designed a bilingual wedding invitation, had it printed, and sent it out to friends and relations all over the world.

Then Edel went to the registry office in Dusseldorf and learned that there were no free slots for a civil wedding before that date. After the stress of taking care of the paperwork, some of it required by only one of the three nations involved, Edel now faced what seemed to be an insurmountable obstacle. She did the only thing she was capable of doing at that point: she broke down and cried. The registrar softened and said that if we were there one-half-hour before normal opening time on the day before our planned church wedding, then he would perform the ceremony.

The appointed day arrived. I had traveled to Dusseldorf the day before. The two of us were at the registrar's on time, along with two witnesses she had organized, but then it turned out that one of them, one of her co-workers in the Editorial Department, had forgotten his identity card. The registrar could have turned us away, but called the registry in our witness's neighborhood and verified his identity, so the ceremony could proceed.

Ceremony over, we set out for the six-hour trip to Niebüll. One of the members of the Brussels congregation had loaned me one of his cars, a vintage Volkswagen Beetle. It wasn't the fastest, we were regularly overtaken on the Autobahn, but we made it. It was so old that it signaled a turn by thrusting out a little flag, rather than having a taillight blink. We wondered why other drivers seemed aggravated at us. It turned out this signal system was no longer permitted on German roads.

That evening, her brother Wolfgang, who was to be my best man, stayed with me in the home of another Worldwide member in Niebüll, while Edel stayed with her parents.

The next day, I donned my white dinner jacket and black tie and went with Wolfgang to the hall in Bargum, where both ceremony and dinner would be held. The service was staged in an Anglo-Saxon way, not continental

European. Wolfgang escorted his mother to a place of honor, and then took his place with Frank Schnee and me in front. Victor Root, the young minister at whose wedding I had danced with Edel the previous summer, played the "Gates of Kiev" from Mussorgsky's *Pictures at an Exhibition* on an electric keyboard, which didn't have quite the effect that I had envisioned when I chose this for our wedding march. Then Edel appeared veiled and in white, holding a bouquet of roses, on the arm of her father. That's my last clear memory of the ceremony. In those days, there was a standard ceremony based on one written by Herbert Armstrong that all ministers used. I used it many times myself in subsequent years; otherwise, I would have no idea what was said that day.

There are memories though of the celebration afterward. There were three groups of guests: relations of mine from the Lintig area, relations of Edel from the local area, and members of the Hamburg congregation supplemented by workers from the Dusseldorf office. One of Edel's Bricket Wood classmates had a private pilot's license, and he flew over with some other students. By the end of the evening, all three contingents had mingled in a warm-hearted way, spurred on by Frank Schnee, who was the life of the party.

Some memories stand out because they were mishaps. One of Edel's uncles was a baker, and he created a many-tiered wedding cake that was leaning as precariously as the tower of Pisa by the time we cut it. And one of the office workers, who had previously owned a camera shop, offered to be our wedding photographer. Something malfunctioned in her camera, though, so we have very few photos, all of them snapshots taken by guests.

Edel and I got away as soon as we could, but not early enough to keep our hotel room. Wolfgang had made the reservation but neglected to inform the hotel that it was our wedding night and that we would likely arrive late. There was only one room left at the hotel, with two single beds attached lengthwise to the wall. The only thing the receptionist could do for us was to send a complementary bottle of champagne to the room.

Maria, my uncle Herman's widow, who split the year between New Jersey and Africa, where her grown children lived, came the farthest, and I seated her to my left at dinner, where my mom would have sat had she been there. My parents, reasonably enough, had decided not to come. Their thinking was that they would have little chance to see us, given all that would be going on. Instead, they sent us the money that their flights would have cost, and we flew to New Jersey a month later, combined with a trip to the Feast of Tabernacles. This caused Edel some apprehension. Meeting my parents would have been one thing, but they planned a party for the entire family; she was faced with over twenty new people at once. "What if they don't like me?" she asked. To which I replied, "Well, it's too late."

For the feast, mindful of Dibar Apartian's reproachful

"where were you?" when he saw me at Bricket Wood after the previous year's feast, we knew we should attend a French-language site, so we drove to Lac Beauport, Qué. Our trip through New York State was Edel's first exposure to New England fall foliage. In Europe, the birch leaves turn pale yellow and the beech golden-bronze. She had never seen anything like a hillside of maples and others in a red and orange blaze.

But that lay a month in the future. Before that, after a spartan, under-planned honeymoon, with Edel making me hot toddies to nurse a bad cold, we settled in as a married couple in the office in Brussels. We had thought of renting our own apartment, but the results of my search were the same as the year before. It made more sense, both for our personal budget and for that of the church, for us to continue to split the rent. Edel didn't mind sharing our home. She hadn't had a room of her own when young; for many years, she slept on the sofa in the living room.

Soon I noticed potted house plants and flowers throughout the apartment. That, and the quality of regular, home-cooked meals, was a change from my bachelor existence. When we married, I was the better cook but had rarely cooked for myself. Edel's mother was an excellent cook but hadn't taught her daughter much about how to do it. I had a similar experience. I learned little about repairing machinery, despite my dad's expertise and my delight in fetching his tools. On the other hand, he was generous in sharing baking and cooking tips when we worked side by side in the delicatessen, and I was an avid learner.

Worldwide emphasized gender roles. Both true masculinity and femininity were under attack, it seems, by women's lib and other social ills. Men were breadwinners, women were homemakers. Nevertheless, I told Edel I didn't mind if she wanted to continue to work after we married. Had we been living near the Dusseldorf office, she probably would have. But she said she would like to try being a homemaker, and found enough to occupy herself all day. We also tried at first to follow other Worldwide expectations, such as studying the Bible together (the man expected to lead). We started with Psalms, but it felt artificial. We left it off after a while without expressly saying we were dropping the idea.

As the end of December approached, we looked forward to having a few quiet days together over the Christmas/New Year break. Not that we would celebrate them, per the church's rejection of what it viewed as pagan rites. Instead, we used the time to add some furniture to our home. We bought a sideboard, a dining table, and chairs in unpainted wood from Galeries Anspach. Danièle wrote instructions for how to stain the wood with roasted, ground walnut shells, after which we rubbed in warm linseed oil. We spread newspaper over the dining room floor and set to work. We had fun working together as a team and then having something to show for it by the time I resumed